THE BEATLES' MERSEYSIDE

Ian Forsyth

For Anna and Sarah

First published in 1991 by S.B. Publications
c/o 19 Grove Road, Seaford, East Sussex BN25 1TP

Reprinted in 1995 (twice)
Revised & Reprinted 1997

© Copyright 1991 Ian Forsyth

British Library Cataloguing in Publication Data

Forsyth, Ian
The Beatles' Merseyside.
I. Title
784.500922

ISBN 1 870708 85 7

Typeset and printed by MFP Design & Print, Longford Trading Estate,
Thomas Street, Stretford, Manchester M32 0JT
Tel: 0161–864 4540

CONTENTS

THE AUTHOR

Ian Forsyth was born in Liverpool and has lived in or near the city all his life. He is an acknowledged authority on the Beatles' early career and has contributed material to various books, magazines and radio programmes about the band.

ACKNOWLEDGEMENTS

All photographs by Willem Eveleens-Maarse or the author.

Anna Forsyth, Marjorie Smith, Willem Eveleens-Maarse, Colin Hanton, Bill Mason, Carl Fletcher, the staff of Beatles Unlimited (The Netherlands), Tommy Mather, Pete Dennett, John Duff Lowe, Sam Leach, Johnny 'Guitar' Byrne, Chris Kelly, Len Garry, Rod Davis, Hilary Coram, Pat Delaney, Johnny Gentle, Carol Higgins and of course the people of Merseyside.

Frank Rhodes of Lightwood, for editing and proof-reading this book.

Special thanks to Steve Benz of S.B. Publications.

BIBLIOGRAPHY

Carroll B. et al. *Liverpool - The Book,* Woodrust, 1989.
Coleman R. *Brian Epstein - The Man Who Made the Beatles,* Viking, 1989.
Coleman R. *John Winston Lennon,* Sidgwick and Jackson, 1984.
Davis H. *The Beatles,* William Heinemann, 1968.
Forsyth I. *Across the Universe - The Beatles,* Proteus Books (Unpublished), 1985.
Goldman A. *The Lives of John Lennon,* Bantam, 1988.
Lennon C. *A Twist of Lennon,* Star Books, 1978.
McCartney M. *Mike McCartney's Family Album,* Arthur Baker, 1981.

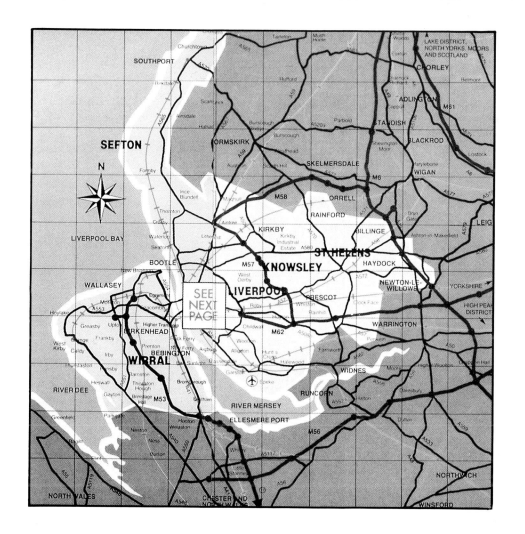

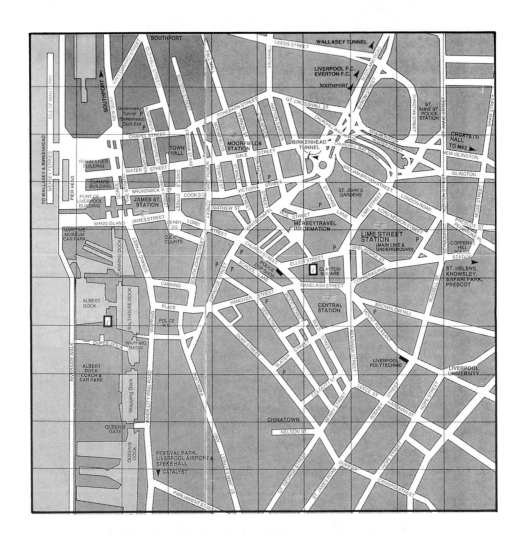

ⓂMerseyrail

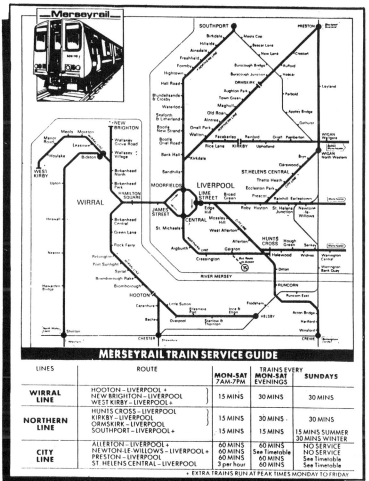

MERSEYRAIL TRAIN SERVICE GUIDE

LINES	ROUTE	MON-SAT 7AM-7PM	TRAINS EVERY MON-SAT EVENINGS	SUNDAYS
WIRRAL LINE	HOOTON – LIVERPOOL + NEW BRIGHTON – LIVERPOOL WEST KIRBY – LIVERPOOL +	15 MINS	30 MINS	30 MINS
NORTHERN LINE	HUNTS CROSS – LIVERPOOL KIRKBY – LIVERPOOL ORMSKIRK – LIVERPOOL SOUTHPORT – LIVERPOOL +	15 MINS 15 MINS	30 MINS 15 MINS	30 MINS 15 MINS SUMMER 30 MINS WINTER
CITY LINE	ALLERTON – LIVERPOOL + NEWTON-LE-WILLOWS – LIVERPOOL + PRESTON – LIVERPOOL ST. HELENS CENTRAL – LIVERPOOL	60 MINS 60 MINS 60 MINS 3 per hour	60 MINS See Timetable 60 MINS 60 MINS	NO SERVICE NO SERVICE See Timetable See Timetable

+ EXTRA TRAINS RUN AT PEAK TIMES MONDAY TO FRIDAY

THE BEATLES' MERSEYSIDE

The Beatles played at the Liverpool Empire Theatre, as part of their British Winter Tour, on 5 December 1965, and as a group they never returned. Less than a year later they had stopped making live appearances altogether. They had tired of it, had become rich beyond their dreams, and possessed the four most famous faces in the world.

Between July 1957 and January 1962, with a few excursions to Germany, they had played the youth clubs, dance halls and nightclubs of Liverpool and the surrounding area. This had been six years of hard slog, with hardly a break, sometimes playing two or three venues a day. It was an exhausting and punishing lifestyle for four teenagers who had little idea of where they were going. After all, it was not until 1962 that they signed a management contract. However, something kept the band going, and after their first trip to Hamburg in August 1960, their popularity increased with each gig. They were helped by an army of friends like former art student Bill Harry, who endeavoured to get them into nearly every issue of his popular local newspaper *Merseybeat*. Bob Wooler, the articulate and very likeable Cavern DJ, took to describing the band as legends as early as 1961. Pete Best's mother, Mona, worked tirelessly to find them recognition and work. The early fan club organisers arranged the special 'Beatle Party Nights' at the Cavern. Neil Aspinall gave up his job to become their 'roadie', and the ever-growing legion of fans showed unflinching loyalty. By 1963 The Beatles had become unstoppable, and would have subsequently made it without Brian Epstein, George Martin, EMI Records and Dick James. They would not, however, have become the massive musical legend they are without each other. Once described as four parts of the whole, each was compatible with the next, but not complete without the other three.

It took five years to find the right formula, with many different line-ups being tried along the way. John and Paul were the nucleus, finding each other way back in 1957. In 1958 George joined. The three then had to wait another four years before Richard 'Ringo' Starkey joined them on drums. From that very day, The Beatles accelerated into the fast lane. Within twelve months they had had two number one records and a number one album, completed three nationwide tours, appeared on dozens of TV and radio programmes, secured a US record distribution deal, played four short summer seasons at British seaside resorts and made their last and two-hundred-and-seventy-second appearance at the Cavern. They were on the brink of world fame, and Liverpool no longer figured in their plans. It was gone but not forgotten.

Very little tangible evidence survives of The Beatles in Liverpool, apart from some faded black-and-white photographs, a grainy television film of a Cavern performance and some early amateur tape recordings. However, there are many memories, and plenty of people to re-tell them. Thirty years on, though, their accuracy must be questionable. What does remain are many of the places that were part of their lives way back then.

Contrary to public myth, they never forgot their home town, and all four Beatles have actively contributed to its growth, through various projects, and by singing its praises at every opportunity. In fact to most people throughout the world, the names Beatles and Liverpool are synonymous. *Strawberry Fields Forever, Penny Lane* and *In My Life* are anthems to their youth and their city, while other songs contain references only decipherable to those born with the sound of the one o'clock gun.

Five years after leaving his home town, Paul's pronounced accent on *Ob La Di Ob La Da* announced to the world that, not only had he retained his accent and humour, but he was fiercely proud of them. The title of the song John wrote for Ringo in 1974, *Goodnight Vienna*, comes from a Liverpool saying meaning, 'Let's get out of here.' In 1976, Paul's *She's My Baby* used 'mopping it up', a local colloquialism for copulation, and in 1984, the title of George's song *Wreck Of The Hesperus* was directly taken from a local saying, meaning 'I look wrecked.'

Over the last twenty years, all four Beatles have been spotted dozens of times in the city or its suburbs: Paul having a glass of wine in Bebington, John and Yoko driving slowly down Mathew Street: George and wife Olivia knocking on the door at 12, Arnold Grove: and Ringo enjoying the sunshine along Otterspool promenade.

The city centre today has changed a lot since the 1960s, and many buildings have been levelled in the name of progress. The beautiful David Lewis Theatre, scene of the very first Beatles Fan Club Night on 17 October 1961, has gone. The Beatles headquarters, the Cavern Club, has long since departed. The Rialto Ballroom on Upper Parliament Street, where producer John Schroeder recorded twenty-three Liverpool bands for the Oriole album *Merseybeat* in 1963, and where The Beatles played a gig for the University in 1962, was burned down during the riots in 1981. (It was around this time that the area known as The Dingle became nationally infamous as Toxteth).

The much-loved Mardi Gras Club was demolished to build a multi-storey car park, and across the Mersey the New Brighton Tower burned down mysteriously in 1969. Even the waterfront's Royal Liver Buildings have been sandblasted, losing the pitch-black look evident on early Beatles publicity photographs. In fact, the actual Liver Birds themselves are now in danger, as the city council wishes to replace them with a newer image, tempting the local legend that if the Liver Birds leave, the city will fall.

The legendary Cast Iron Shore, with its grimy beach and labyrinthine caves, has metamorphosed into the Garden Festival Site. The Wilson Hall in Garston is a carpet centre, and the Abbey Cinema is now a supermarket.

Fortunately the city has been preserved in some fine evocative films shot in the city over the last forty years. *Violent Playground (1957)* starring Stanley Baker, *Dangerous Youth (1958)* and *The Magnet (1950)* starring a very young James Fox, capture accurately the Liverpool of the fifties. If you watch the oddly-titled thriller *I Thank A Fool (1962)* featuring Susan Heywood and Peter Finch, New Brighton Tower can be seen clearly in several background shots. *Ferry Across The Mersey (1965)* had location filming at the Cavern, the Grafton Rooms, Frank Hessy's music shop and the Mersey ferry boats, and later films, such as *Gumshoe (1972), Letter To Brezhnev (1984)* and *The Fruit Machine (1988)* have recorded the city's humour, atmosphere and decay.

The tenements of The Dingle, Caryl and Myrtle Gardens, Upper Parliament Street, whose Georgian houses and basements contained the shebeens and strip clubs of the fifties and sixties, have been demolished in favour of row upon row of neat public housing. (The Beatles backed Janice, a stripper from Manchester, in a basement club off Upper Parliament Street in 1960). The area of little streets surrounding the Anglican Cathedral, Washington Street, Nile Street and Sand Street, once the haunt of 'The Black Hand Gang' in the twenties and thirties, and collectively known as St James, is now a new private estate of small expensive houses.

Nearly all the city centre clubs The Beatles knew have disappeared in the last twenty years: The Downbeat: The Iron Door: Hope Hall: The Rumblin' Tum: The Sink: The Temple: The Peppermint Lounge: The Oslo and The Cavern. Back in the sixties, the eight miles of docks were mostly operational, although some south end docks had been abandoned. The Albert Dock remained dormant for years. Herculaneum, one of the oldest, and lying below the tiny terraced houses of The Dingle, where BBC TV's *Bread* is now filmed, lay useless. The last tram ran in 1958, and the overhead railway, also known as 'The Dockers' Umbrella' because of its value to stevedores as a shelter on wet days, was demolished the same year. The latter was featured in the original lyrics of Lennon's *In My Life*.

Years of neglect have signed the death warrant of many a fine building. Paul's old school, the Liverpool Institute, was in such a state by the mid-eighties that it had to be closed down.

Exiles returning to the city after twenty years would be baffled by the one-way system, and would the absurd new 'Famous Mersey Ferries', complete with commentary and Beatles music, make them laugh or cry? Other modes of transport have both suffered and improved. The once excellent bus system is now unfathomable. Readers using buses to visit the places in this book will need patience. Forewarned is forearmed. The trains, however, are excellent. Many old stations have been spruced up and re-opened, making it easy and pleasurable to criss-cross the length and breadth of Merseyside.

Incidentally, Merseyside is now a fully-fledged county. In the sixties, Liverpool was in the county of Lancashire, but after the re-organisation of the counties in 1974, when Britain lost, among others, its smallest county, Rutland, many outlying towns and villages came under the collective 'Nuclear Free' County of Merseyside. Many new Merseysiders did not want what they regarded as a dubious new status, but the problem was solved when the Post Office agreed that they could continue to use the old county in their address.

Fortunately, the suburbs have hardly changed at all. The Beatles birth-places are still standing, as are nearly all their subsequent homes and schools. The pubs and cafes, cinemas, clubs, churches and dance halls are still there. The 'shelter in the middle of a roundabout', where John and Paul waited for buses in Penny Lane, still serves a useful purpose. St Peter's Church still has its annual fete, and the Church Hall its Christmas Fair. Woolton is still very much a village where everyone knows everyone else, and many still remember Mimi Smith and her young nephew, John.

Until recently, Liverpool made little of its Beatles connections. In fact, even now Beatles fans are not exactly numerous. Many people are still angry they left, believing somehow that they should have stayed where they were, refusing steadfastly what the rest of the world was offering. Nevertheless, fifty thousand people turned out on a summer night in 1990, to see Paul McCartney when his world tour finally arrived in his home town, after a gruelling one hundred dates. That is nearly ten per cent of the city's population, and if the average Liverpool home has five occupants, then half the homes in Liverpool had a representative at the concert on that magical June night. Should George or Ringo ever decide to play his home town, a similar welcome would be waiting for him.

Liverpool has traditionally been split into two camps, the North End and the South End. An imaginary line, drawn east from the Pier Head across to Huyton, divides the two. All four Beatles are South Enders, and most of the places in the following pages are found in the southern half of the city. To make sense of the one hundred and twelve locations, they have been grouped into twelve sections, ten being areas of the city, whilst the other two cover the nearby Wirral and the outlying towns. (That is towns within a twenty-mile radius).

Readers who plan to visit all the places should tackle it using the sections, an up-to-date A-Z of the city (available from any good bookshop or newsagent), and allowing themselves a full week. Use of a car is ideal, and obviously cuts down on time. If the only choice is public transport, then one must allow for time spent waiting. For those with less time or tenacity, an abbreviated tour is printed at the end of the book. A map for these is available from The Beatles Shop in Mathew Street, The Beatles Story in The Albert Dock Complex or from the Merseyside Tourist Board. It should be remembered that all the places are private property. Present owners do not want to be harassed, and just because someone lives in a former home of a Beatle, it does not follow that they knew, or know, The Beatles.

School authorities take a dim view of trespassers, which is hardly surprising, since they are responsible for the safety of the children in their care. On no account should anyone enter the grounds of the children's home, Strawberry Field, so please be content to view from a respectable distance. Merseysiders are a friendly lot, who will go to extraordinary lengths to put the traveller on the right road, so don't be afraid to ask, should you become totally lost, or just need some help with the A-Z.

Because this is the 1990s, and not the 1960s, it is wise to mention personal safety. In common with other large cities, Liverpool has its share of dangerous characters, and there are places where strangers should not venture after nightfall. Exhibiting money and expensive cameras might be an invitation to a thief. If this is beginning to sound depressing, it should be remembered that these unscrupulous characters are the exception and not the rule.

For advice on nightclubs and the different areas of Liverpool and their varying degrees of safety, the city's taxi drivers are a mine of information. The much-maligned black cabs are driven by salt-of-the-earth people whose quirky philosophy and humour is unrivalled, even by the legendary yellow-cab drivers of New York City.

Since The Beatles went their separate ways in 1970, hundreds of books have been written about them, and undoubtedly there will be hundreds more as new generations discover them. Every aspect has been covered, from the basic story to the more esoteric discographies. There have even been a couple of Beatles guides to Liverpool, and while they were useful, they were far from comprehensive, and the travel information either non-existent or unfathomable. Hopefully, this book will cover previous omissions, and be useful to travellers and armchair visitors alike. It will give the reader a taste of the city, and allow him to travel back in time to see what it was like when The Beatles could be hired for £10.00 - all in.

As John Lennon once said, 'You should have been there!'

THE PIER HEAD

Here is an obvious place to begin, and an important landmark when looking at The Beatles antecedents. Once the berthing-place of the great transatlantic liners of Cunard and Canadian Pacific and the busy Irish and Welsh boats, it is now the domain only of the Mersey ferries. Although of Scottish origin, the McCartneys arrived here after a century of farming in Northern Ireland. Jack Lennon, later to become a Kentucky Minstrel, and whose son Alfred would sail from the port regularly in the twenties and thirties, arrived from Dublin in the late 1800s. George's father, Harold Harrison, was once a 'Cunard Yank' serving on the transatlantic liners in the thirties. In 1945, Johnny, Mona and Pete Best disembarked from India, and a decade later sixteen-year-old Ringo Starr worked as a waiter on the *St Tudno*, the North Wales pleasure-steamer. More recently, on 5 May 1990, a concert was held on the windswept square at the front of The Royal Liver Buildings in memory of John Lennon. It was organised by his widow Yoko Ono, and featured a host of music stars including his youngest son Sean.

THE BEATLES STORY, BRITANNIA VAULTS, ALBERT DOCK
This is Liverpool's only permanent Beatles Exhibition, and opens from 10.00 am until 6.00 pm seven days a week. Described as 'a walk-through experience', the exhibition is separated into various sections: the Star Club: Mathew Street: Beatlemania: Yellow Submarine: etc.. Older fans will probably have seen most of it before, but there are some interesting posters, photographs and contracts. There is also a souvenir shop at the end of the tour.

For further details telephone 051-709-1963.

THE KING'S DOCK ARENA, ADJACENT TO ALBERT DOCK
Three hundred yards south of the Albert Dock complex is the site of what was the King's Dock Arena. Here on the evening of 28 June 1990, Paul McCartney played to fifty thousand ecstatic Scousers, in his first world tour for thirteen years. The concert, in aid of charities including Alder Hey Children's Hospital and the Marie Curie Centre, cost so much to stage that it only broke even, so Paul paid £100,000 of his own money to avoid any loss to the charities. Unfortunately, the concert was the only one held at the King's Dock, and it has now reverted to its original use as an overspill car park for the Albert Dock complex.

KINGSTON HOTEL, STRAND STREET (ONCE MERCHANT NAVY BUILDING)

While waiting for the autumn term to start at art school, John Lennon and friend Nigel Whalley decided to sign on the seamen's register here, some time in July 1957. John may have been drawn to the life his father had chosen, or he may have been just bored. Whatever the reason, the idea was soon nipped in the bud by Mimi who as his legal guardian refused to sign the necessary papers for the sixteen-year-old would-be matelot.

RADIO MERSEYSIDE, PARADISE STREET

Radio Merseyside began broadcasting from its studios in Sir Thomas Street in 1967. In December 1981, they moved to their present location in Paradise Street. Several of the station's staff have Merseybeat connections. Kenny Johnson was formerly Sonny Webb of Sonny Webb and the Cascades, Billy Butler was a DJ at the Cavern from 1964, and Bob Azurdia was the first British journalist to write about The Beatles in a national paper. Paul has recorded several interviews for Merseyside. Of the two most memorable, the first broadcast on 23 April 1984, concerned his solo debut in *Give My Regards To Broad Street*, and the second, broadcast on 23 June 1990, centred around his return home to a Liverpool concert at the King's Dock arena on 28 June 1990. In 1986, Paul sent £8000 to the station's 'Children In Need' charity appeal. Spencer Leigh, by far the most knowledgeable presenter, is a great Beatles fan, and has produced some fine programmes, including *On The Beat,* and the wonderful 1981 twelve-part documentary series about Merseybeat, *Let's Go Down The Cavern*.

BLUECOAT CHAMBERS, SCHOOL LANE

This grade I listed Georgian building has only tentative links with The Beatles. It was originally an orphanage, before the boys were moved to Bluecoat School in Church Road, Wavertree. John's father, Alfred Lennon, was a Bluecoat boy. Later, it became a library, then an arts centre. In September 1967, avant-garde artist Yoko Ono, then married to Tony Cox, was paid £30.00 by the Bluecoat to stage a 'happening'. Twenty-eight years after the death in Hamburg of Stuart Sutcliffe, the Bluecoat hosted his first major exhibition in Liverpool, between July and September 1990.

LIVERPOOL TOWN HALL, WATER STREET

On 10 July 1964, The Beatles returned to Liverpool for an official civic reception at the Town Hall, and the northern premiere of their first feature film, *A Hard Day's Night*. After arriving at Speke Airport they took a slow drive by limousine through the city, with approximately half a million people lining the route. Before being whisked off to the nearby Odeon cinema, John, Paul, George and Ringo appeared on the balcony alongside Lord Mayor Alderman Louis Caplan, to acknowledge the waiting fans below. John could not resist giving a 'Hitler' salute, but such was their popularity that it was not mentioned in the following day's press. Paul returned to Liverpool on 28 November 1984, to be awarded the honour of Freeman of the City. This entitles him 'to unsheath his sword within the city boundaries.' The building dates back to 1754, and the dome bears the city's motto: *DEUS NOBIS HAEC OTIA FECIT* (God has provided for us this leisure).

THE IRON DOOR CLUB, 13, TEMPLE STREET

The Iron Door Club was originally known as the Storreyville Jazz Club, and was the home of the Liverpool Jazz Society. The Beatles played for the society on 13 March 1961. How they were received is not known, but they did return two days later. They played their third and final gig at the Storreyville a year later, on 6 March 1962. By 1963 the club had become the Iron Door, and if the Cavern was The Beatles headquarters, then the Iron Door was home to that other greatly influential Liverpool band, The Searchers. The club did actually have an iron door. The old wooden one was replaced after a gang, hot in pursuit of Derry Wilkie (of Derry Wilkie and The Seniors) attacked it with axes. The police arrived before the gang could gain entry, and Derry survived.

CAVERN WALKS, MATHEW STREET

The original Cavern Club was opened in the basement of a fruit warehouse at 10 Mathew Street on 16 January 1957 and enjoyed a chequered history, playing host to hundreds of top jazz and rock musicians, before closing finally on 27 May 1973. The Beatles played the Cavern twice as The Quarrymen in 1957, before becoming regulars after their official debut in February 1961. Between then and 3 August 1963, they put in two hundred and seventy-two appearances. There exists a couple of tapes of them at the Cavern, and in 1962, Granada TV filmed them performing *Some Other Guy* and *Kansas City*. Unfortunately the resultant film quality was poor. For a better sample of Cavern atmosphere it is worth listening to the Decca LP *At The Cavern* (LK 4597) compered by Bob Wooler, and featuring, among others, the superlative Big Three, whose own EP *The Big Three Live At The Cavern* (DFE 8552) also gives a good impression of those halcyon days.

9

CAVERN WALKS, MATHEW STREET

In October 1982, major property developer Royal Life, whose headquarters are in Liverpool, started construction of their ambitious project, Cavern Walks, nine years after the original warehouse had been bulldozed. Although the cellar club itself had only been filled in with the resultant rubble, Royal Life found the original Cavern beneath the debris, but decided to dismantle it. They kept most of the club's original bricks, selling some at £5.00 each for charity, and using the remainder in the replica built several yards to the right. Overall a good reconstruction was done, and the visitor is left in no doubt of The Beatles connection, from the John Doubleday bronze busts outside to the action statues inside, next to the Abbey Road Pub.

**GRAPES PUBLIC HOUSE,
MATHEW STREET**
Because of the Cavern's policy of
selling only soft drinks, most of the
musicians including The Beatles,
made their way to the Grapes for
something a bit stronger. Even today,
famous people from the Merseybeat
era can be seen and heard in the
Grapes, re-living past glories.

WHITE STAR PUBLIC HOUSE, RAINFORD GARDENS

Just across the road from the Grapes, and famous for its draught Bass, this would have been an alternative watering hole for thirsty members of the group. The public house takes its name from the White Star Line Shipping Company, which later merged with Cunard; the new company was known as Cunard White Star. George Harrison's father was at one time a steward with White Star. The company announced the sinking of *Titanic* from its red-and-white striped headquarters which can still be seen in James Street, opposite the Old Seamen's Mission.

HESSY'S MUSIC SHOP,
(NOW WADE SMITH JNR)
STANLEY STREET

Early in 1957, after constant haranguing from her sixteen-year-old nephew, who was obsessed with rock 'n roll, Mimi Smith capitulated and bought him an acoustic guitar for fourteen pounds from the shop of Frank Hessy. Nearly five years later, in December 1961, Brian Epstein met Hessy's manager, Bernard Michaelson, with the intention of paying off the group's HP debts. He was unshaken when told that the amount was nearly £200 and cleared the debt immediately with a personal cheque. For those interested, in 1961 John was playing a Hofner 126/B, George a Gretsch Duo Jet PX 6128 and Paul a Hofner Bass 500/1. Sadly Hessy's closed in 1995 and is now a clothes shop.

**ELEANOR RIGBY,
STANLEY STREET**
Early British rocker turned all-round entertainer, Tommy Steele sculpted and donated this statue to the city for 'half a sixpence', as a tribute to The Beatles in December 1982. It is reputed to have cost him £4000. The bronze casting of the Beatles character is seated on a bench frequently used by couples eating take-aways after a night on the town. It is dedicated to 'all the lonely people.'

RUSHWORTHS MUSIC HOUSE, WHITECHAPEL
During the sixties, Rushworth's competed with NEMS and Beaver Radio for the title of Liverpool's
largest record store. However, it was probably better known, and still is, for selling quality musical
instruments. The Beatles, and hundreds of other musicians, bought guitars, strings and plectrums
at Rushworth's. In 1962, the then manager, Bob Hobbs, presented George and John with guitars,
following the band's success in the Merseybeat Poll.

NEMS, WHITECHAPEL (NOW ANN SUMMERS)

Here we have the 1960s headquarters of NEMS Ltd. NEMS was an acronym for North End Music Stores, whose first shop had been in Walton. There was another city branch in Great Charlotte Street and half a dozen smaller branches throughout Merseyside. Brian Epstein's father, Harry, started the company in the thirties, and Brian took over the helm in the late fifties. There is a well-known legend that some time in 1961, Brian was asked for a copy of the German record *My Bonnie* by Tony Sheridan and The Beatbrothers. He then found that The Beatles (Beatbrothers) were a local band, playing in a basement a stone's throw from his shop. With his assistant Alistair Taylor, he visited the Cavern, and the rest is history. It has since been pointed out by Bill Harry, editor and publisher of the local beat bible *Merseybeat*, that Brian knew of the popularity of The Beatles much earlier. In view of the amount of front-page publicity he gave them, it does seem improbable that Brian was unaware of them until late 1961. It is claimed that above the existing false ceiling in the store, Brian's original display of early sixties album covers is still intact.

THE ROYAL COURT THEATRE, ROE STREET

The poor relation in Liverpool theatre land, the Royal Court has had a chequered history of near-closure, only to be saved at the last minute. In the fifties and sixties it presented variety shows, Christmas pantomime and drama. Brian Epstein saw nearly every performance given by Vivien Leigh at the Royal Court. More recently it has become a rock venue, and on 23 November 1979, Paul McCartney, with what was to be his final Wings line-up, opened his British tour here. He played a special concert for invited guests and all the pupils of his old school, The Institute. Even his old headmaster attended and joined the backstage party afterwards. The following three nights saw three more sell-out concerts for Wings before the tour moved on to Manchester. On 3 July 1989, Julian Lennon joined other musicians for a charity gig at the Royal Court, for the bereaved families of the Hillsborough disaster.

BLACKLER'S DEPARTMENT STORE, GREAT CHARLOTTE STREET
In the summer of 1959, George left the Institute with no academic qualifications. He tried to obtain an apprenticeship with Liverpool Corporation, but failed the entrance examination. The Youth Employment Office sent him here to seek a job as a window-dresser. Unfortunately the vacancy had been filled, but he was offered an electrical apprenticeship. He spent most of his short time at Blackler's playing darts and dreaming of emigrating. Eventually, he abandoned thoughts of Australia and Canada, reasoning that 'something would turn up'.

**LEWIS'S DEPARTMENT
STORE, RANELAGH STREET**
With Jacob Epstein's nude male statue
towering above the front entrance, this
is probably the most famous store in
Liverpool. It is a well-known
meeting-place for courting couples,
including John and Cynthia. In 1959,
after Paul left school, he worked for
Lewis's for a short time as a driver's
assistant, delivering customers'
orders. The Beatles played at a
Christmas dance for the staff
immediately after an early evening
Cavern gig on 28 November 1962.

THE BRITANNIA ADELPHI, RANELAGH PLACE

Once described as 'a great Cunard liner stranded in the middle of the city', the Adelphi is probably Liverpool's most famous hotel. Scores of rich and famous people, including The Beatles, Bob Dylan and Gregory Peck, have stayed here. On 3 December 1938, Freddie Lennon and Julia Stanley met on the steps outside, before making their way to the Bolton Street Registry Office. After the short ceremony, Freddie's brother Sydney bought lunch and drinks at a nearby public house, before the newlyweds left to spend the afternoon at the cinema. Nowadays the annual Beatles convention, the largest in the world, is held at the Adelphi, usually during the last week of August.

EMPIRE THEATRE, LIME STREET

The largest regional theatre in the country, with a seating capacity of 2312, it was originally part of the Moss Empires chain. Mimi used to take John to the pantomime every Christmas, and on one occasion, in company with some other children, he was invited by the good fairy to come to the front of the stage. On reaching the lady, he shouted back to Mimi, 'She's not a very young fairy, Mimi.' The Quarrymen auditioned for 'Carrol Levis Discoveries' at the Empire in 1957, and returned to try again in 1959. Nothing came of the auditions, but as The Beatles they went on to play the theatre a further seven times. The 1963 BBC TV special *It's The Beatles* was recorded here on 7 December at a concert organised by the Northern Area Fan Club. The group tried out their Christmas Show on 22 December 1963, before opening it two days later at the Finsbury Park Astoria, where it enjoyed a three-week run. In the seventies, Paul played the Empire three times, twice on 18 May 1973 and once on 15 September 1975.

ST GEORGE'S HALL, LIME STREET

In 1959, Allan Williams, after visiting the Chelsea Arts Ball, decided to organise a similar event here at one of Liverpool's most impressive buildings. He recruited the under-employed John, Paul, George and Stuart to help build some of the floats. Unfortunately, the high spirits got out of hand and the evening ended in chaos. The City Council decided it would not be allowed again. At 7.00pm on 14 December 1980, ten thousand fans, joining a simultaneous vigil worldwide, gathered below the sixty-foot high Corinthian columns, to pay their respects to the memory of John Lennon by observing a short period of silence.

ODEON CINEMA, LONDON ROAD

On 7 December 1963, it was a busy day for The Beatles in their home town. After spending the afternoon filming two BBC television programmes, *It's The Beatles* and *Juke Box Jury*, at the Empire Theatre, they dashed the hundred yards or so through Pudsey Street to the Odeon Cinema to give a further two shows. Seven months later, on 10 July 1964, the cinema hosted the northern premiere of *A Hard Day's Night*. The London world premiere had been four days earlier in the presence of HRH Princess Margaret and Lord Snowdon. Paul returned to the Odeon on 28 November 1984 for the UK premiere of his first solo feature film *Give My Regards to Broad Street*.

**LIVERPOOL REGISTRY OFFICE,
64, MOUNT PLEASANT**

John Lennon married Cynthia Powell here on 23 August 1962. Brian Epstein was best man and the guests were Paul McCartney, George Harrison and Cynthia's sister-in-law Marjorie Powell. After the ceremony, they had their wedding breakfast at Reeces' Restaurant in Parker Street, and John spent his wedding night playing with The Beatles at The Riverpark Ballroom in Chester.

EX-MATERNITY HOSPITAL, OXFORD STREET

Contrary to Beatles legend, the Luftwaffe was not bombing Liverpool when John Lennon was born on 9 October 1940. John's mother Julia had been in labour for almost thirty-six hours, and doctors were considering a Caesarian section when the blonde-haired, seven-and-a-half pound baby arrived. Aunt Mimi arrived after being given the news by telephone and confronted her future charge for the first time. 'I knew the moment I first set eyes on John that he was going to be something special.'

EVERYMAN THEATRE, HOPE STREET

This theatre, which opened in 1964, has built a reputation for being daring, innovative and controversial. Two Beatles plays have had their world premieres at the Everyman, before moving on to London and New York: in 1974, Willy Russell's *John, Paul, George, Ringo and Bert,* which starred ex-Rebel Arthur Kelly as Bert: and in 1982, Bob Eaton's celebration of John's life *Lennon.*

THE PHILHARMONIC HOTEL, HOPE STREET

This is one of the city's most interesting public houses and shares the same name as the Philharmonic Hall directly opposite (home of the world-renowned Liverpool Philharmonic Orchestra). Because of its close proximity to the Art College and The Institute, it is quite likely that The Beatles quaffed a pint or two in its Victorian bars. It really is a curio and is well worth a visit for its own sake.

YE CRACKE PUBLIC HOUSE, RICE STREET

Situated near the university and the polytechnic, this has long been a students' haunt. It was in the tiny back room that John and Stuart talked earnestly of Van Gogh and Jackson Pollock, and love blossomed between John and Cynthia. One of the nicest stories Cyn tells of those days is of a particularly hot day, when they and some friends were standing outside the pub and film actor John Gregson drew up in his new sports car. Having asked the star of *Genevieve* for his autograph, they found they had no paper for the famous Liverpudlian to sign. Unperturbed, Lennon disappeared for a few minutes and returned, quite straight-faced, with an old leather boot, which a laughing Gregson duly signed, before roaring off up Rice Street.

LIVERPOOL COLLEGE OF ART, MOUNT STREET (Now LIVERPOOL POLYTECHNIC, FACULTY OF ART AND DESIGN)

In June 1957, armed with a hastily-assembled portfolio, and a reference from Quarry Bank's headmaster, William Pobjoy, John Lennon, soberly dressed in a suit belonging to his Uncle George, attended an interview here with the College Principal Mr Stevenson. After nearly an hour Stevenson was sufficiently impressed to offer John a place at the college, starting in September of that year. He reminded John that college life was very different from school. It was largely unsupervised, and the students were expected to complete work on time by their own efforts. All of this must have sounded like heaven to John after the disciplined structure of Quarry Bank, and he certainly enjoyed the life of a student. Stamping his individuality on staff and students alike, he began to attract his own group of followers around him. The Lennon gang consisted of the diminutive and massively talented Stuart Sutcliffe, shy Cheshire girl Cynthia Powell, Anglo-Indian Geoff Mohammed, artists' model June Furlong, Dave Davies, Tony Carrick, Ann Mason and Helen Anderson.

LIVERPOOL COLLEGE OF ART, MOUNT STREET (cont.)

Cartoonist Michael Isaacson, who had been at Quarry Bank, remained unimpressed. Michael was an achiever who was 'printed' by the university in their students' rag magazine, and later by the Liverpool Echo. He saw Lennon unchanged: as a talent, but a waster. If pop music had not saved him, he would have been a bum, an opinion shared by many. In his defence it must be said that his attitude to work was good until his mother was killed. After 15 July 1958, John became a Jekyll and Hyde character, mocking all that was simple and good and reverting to his Quarry Bank personality, as a rebel without a cause. He hated everything and almost everyone for years, and unrelentingly relieved his feelings on all who were close to him. One of the few tutors who were sympathetic, Arthur Ballard, remembers surprising a weeping Lennon on the college staircase one morning. In fact, despite his hard case image, Lennon was saved not by soul-mate Stuart Sutcliffe, but by the caring and totally infatuated Cynthia Powell. Her rural simplicity and total loyalty allowed John to breathe. She wanted nothing from him but his love, and she would remain at his side for another nine years. In May 1960, The Silver Beatles were offered a tour of Scotland's east coast with Johnny Gentle. It took two minutes for John to make the decision to leave art school. He made the right one, as the college had already decided to cut short his studies in July of that year, because his work had not been up to standard for some time.

LIVERPOOL INSTITUTE, MOUNT STREET
(NOW LIVERPOOL INSTITUTE FOR PERFORMING ARTS)

Once one of Liverpool's finest grammar schools, 'The Innie' was forced to close in 1985 after years of neglect. Built in 1825, it was literally falling down. Two Beatles were educated here: Paul between 1953 and 1958, and George from 1954 to 1958. Among their contemporaries were newsreader and journalist Peter Sissons, actor and producer Bill Kenwright, Les Chadwick (later to join Gerry and The Pacemakers) and Ivan Vaughan, a Quarryman who introduced Paul to John in 1957. John's uncle, George Smith (Mimi's husband) had a brother who was a teacher at the Institute. Paul managed to pass five 'O'-levels, three in foreign languages, and encouraged by his English master, Alan 'Dusty' Durband, he entered the sixth form to prepare for 'A'-levels in Art and English. The family hoped he would get a place at a teacher-training college. He was certainly capable of it, but Paul had his mind on other things. He would amaze his father and brother by being able to do his homework, watch television and eat his dinner, all at the same time. Bill Kenwright remembers Paul as a born actor when they were both in a school production of *Saint Joan*. George, on the other hand, was an undistinguished scholar and something of a rebel. He brightened up his school uniform by wearing a canary-yellow waistcoat, and his hair was always worn long. Paul and George have known each other since 1954, as they often shared the same bus to and from their homes in Speke. After John enrolled at the Art College next door to 'The Innie' in 1957, he and Paul often met at lunchtimes, eating in the college's refectory and planning the group's next move. After 1958, when George joined, all three Beatles were able to skip lessons or lectures at a few minutes notice in favour of a group rehearsal.

LIVERPOOL INSTITUTE, MOUNT STREET (cont.)

In 1989 Paul announced that the old Institute building was to become the Liverpool Institute For Performing Arts. Work commenced and funds were raised. On Tuesday 30.1.1996 Paul officially opened LIPA and it is now attended by students from all over the World. Although extensively re-built the Mount Street entrance looks much as it did in the 1950s.

3, GAMBIER TERRACE

John Lennon moved into Stuart Sutcliffe's first-floor flat in this late-Georgian terraced house in early 1960. It is said that he slept in a satin-lined coffin. All The Beatles met, ate and slept at the flat regularly during 1960. The 24 July issue of the Sunday newspaper *The People* carried a story headed 'The Beatnik Horror', and beneath the caption was a photograph of some young men, lying on the floor in Stuart's flat, surrounded by squalor. Amongst them is the unmistakeable face of nineteen-year-old John Lennon. The much-published photograph of John, with a group of student friends, was taken in the terrace's private drive, with the entrance gates in the background.

LIVERPOOL ANGLICAN CATHEDRAL, HOPE STREET

In 1953, eleven-year-old Speke schoolboy James Paul McCartney attended an audition here, hoping for a place in the choir of what is the largest Anglican Cathedral in the world. He was unsuccessful. Ironically in 1991 Paul was commissioned, with Carl Davis, to write an exclusive musical work for the same choir. The resultant LIVERPOOL ORATORIO has now been performed hundred times worldwide. On March 29 1981 a capacity congregation attended a memorial service at the cathedral for John Lennon.

7, PERCY STREET

Before Stuart Sutcliffe moved into Gambier Terrace with his fellow-student Rod Murray, he had his own basement studio here between 1957 and 1959. He often chose to work alone in the studio in preference to attending the art school. Stuart's major influences were the French Impressionists, the English pre-Raphaelites, Jackson Pollock, Nicholas de Stael and Buddy Holly, whose records he played constantly while he painted. In the eighties, builders at work on the roof of nos. 7 and 9 found a stone carving bearing the marks 'JL VB' (John Lennon, class 5B). There was some controversy over its origin before experts declared it fake and consequently valueless.

36, FALKNER STREET

Brian Epstein rented a ground-floor flat here during 1961 and 1962 for £4.00 per week. After John married Cynthia in August 1962, Brian gave them the keys, and the Lennons set up their first home, in the heart of the city's red light district, while searching for a permanent place of their own.

JOE'S CAFE, 139, DUKE STREET

On 1 January 1962, The Beatles auditioned for Decca Records at the company's West Hampstead studio. They were competent, if a little nervous, and they all agreed as they headed home, that they had cracked it. It was not to be, but it took Decca three months before the news was broken to a devastated Epstein. He then had to tell John, Paul, George and Pete; not an easy task, and he told them here, at an all-night cafe, after a Cavern gig. Lennon's reaction was typically ascerbic. After berating his manager of less than five months for his incompetence, he demanded that Brian try Embassy. This was Woolworth's own record label, which specialised in cover-versions of the day's hits. John did not care who published his music, just as long as someone did.

THE WYVERN SOCIAL CLUB, 108, SEEL STREET (LATER THE BLUE ANGEL)

On Tuesday morning, 10 May 1960, half a dozen of Liverpool's top bands arrived at the Wyvern Social Club to audition for leading impresario Larry Parnes, who was looking for a backing group for his brightest star, Billy Fury. The audition was organised by Allan Williams, who had just leased the Wyvern, and because of this, The Beatles had been invited to try their luck. They were very much outsiders, but incredibly they led the field. But for their inept bass player, Stuart, they would have been Billy Fury's next backing band. Almost as a consolation, Parnes offered them an eight-day tour of north-east Scotland, backing another of his stable of rock stars, Johnny Gentle. This was the only occasion that The Beatles played the Wyvern/Blue Angel, although they used the club to relax after Cavern gigs during 1961 and 1962.

THE JACARANDA CLUB, 23, SLATER STREET

Allan Williams opened 'The Jac' as a coffee bar in 1958, basing it loosely on 'The Two I's' in London, where Tommy Steele had been discovered· two years earlier. During the day, John, Paul, George and Stuart drank coffee and ate bacon butties. At night they played amateurish rock 'n roll in the basement for £1.00 each. So short of money were they, that Williams managed to persuade them to paint murals on the walls and even clean the ladies' toilets for a few pounds. Although he thought little of their musical ability he did manage to get them the Larry Parnes audition which resulted in a two week tour with Johnny Gentle in May 1960. That tour's Scottish promoter, Duncan McKinnon, shared Williams' lack of enthusiasm, and if Gentle himself had not insisted on their getting their act together after the second night of the tour, in Inverness, they would have been sacked. Three months later, again thanks to Allan, they were on their way to Hamburg. Sixteen weeks in the St Pauli nightclubs· would transform the amateurish Silver Beatles into Liverpool's hardest rock powerhouse - The Beatles.

THE ODD SPOT CLUB, BOLD STREET

The Beatles only played the Odd Spot twice, on 22 March and 11 August 1962. However, the first occasion is worth a mention. They had just won the Merseybeat Poll and were preparing to fly to Hamburg the following month for a seven-week season. Epstein had now taken full control and he was eager to have some photographs taken of the new image. The old leather gear had gone and had been replaced by tailor-made suits, white shirts and dark ties. Alan Swerdlow, an amateur photographer and friend of Brian, accompanied the band and took twenty-four black and white shots showing The Beatles, still eighteen months away from national Beatlemania, but looking just as they would when that phenomenon exploded. It was now just a matter of time.

THE LYCEUM, BOLD STREET

Built in 1800 as a 'Gentlemen's Club', the Lyceum has had a chequered history and has been saved from the bulldozer more than once. In the sixties, it was a waitress-service cafe. The Beatles regularly took coffee here, and on one occasion scribbled lyrics on some serviettes. The discarded scraps of paper were retrieved by an eagle-eyed waitress, and these valuable pieces of memorabilia turned up later at a Sotheby's Beatles auction in the eighties. The building now belongs to the Post Office, and is at last protected by a grade II listing.

COLLEGIATE GRAMMAR SCHOOL, SHAW STREET

Sadly now derelict, this was once one of the city's finest grammar schools. It was here that Pete Best was educated between 1953 and 1958. Like John, Paul and George, Pete had passed the eleven-plus examination at his Blackmoor Park primary school in West Derby. The building is made of sandstone from the Woolton quarry, a material used also for the Anglican Cathedral.

38, KENSINGTON

It was here at a small commercial recording studio that The Quarrymen cut their one and only record in early 1958. It cost 17s 6d (£0.87½) and only one copy was pressed. On the primitive equipment they did Buddy Holly's *That'll Be The Day* and a McCartney/Harrison original *In Spite Of All The Danger*. During the sixties the 78 rpm disc was lost, only to resurface in 1982 in the possession of John 'Duff' Lowe, who is an ex-Quarryman. Paul quickly negotiated and regained possession at a cost reputed to be £5000. In late 1990, it was rumoured that Paul had had fifty copies made to give to his friends as Christmas presents.

THE GRAFTON/LOCARNO BALLROOMS, WEST DERBY ROAD

These two ballrooms are situated side by side on the outskirts of the city. They have been in business since the thirties, and are legendary. The Quarrymen entered dozens of skiffle talent contests here in the late fifties. The Beatles played both ballrooms many times, the last being at The Grafton on 2.8.1963 for an NSPCC charity dance. Dance hall scenes for the 1965 film *Ferry Across The Mersey* were shot in the Grafton.

9, MADRYN STREET

Birthplace of Richard Starkey, who appeared a week late, a ten-pound baby, at midnight on 7 July 1940, thus making Ringo Starr the oldest Beatle. The house was rented by Mr and Mrs Starkey paying ten shillings (£0.50) a week. Ringo's parents separated three years later, and mother and son moved to a smaller, less expensive house, a stone's throw away in Admiral Grove, some time in 1945.

10, ADMIRAL GROVE

After Ringo's dad, Richard, left Elsie when Ringo was three years old, she found the rent in Madryn Street hard to manage, so they moved into this smaller house in Admiral Grove. It remained Ringo's home until he became nationally famous in 1963. Although Admiral Grove has only four rooms, two up and two down, legend has it that on Ringo's twenty-first birthday, on 7 July 1961, nearly two hundred local musicians and their girlfriends packed into the tiny house for a party. Cilla Black was a friend of Mrs Starkey, and was a frequent visitor to the house. As Ringo was a sickly child who missed much of his schooling, he was taught at home to read and write, by a local girl, Marie Maguire. When Ringo was thirteen, Elsie married a Londoner, Harry Graves, who had come to Liverpool after his doctor suggested that he needed a change of air! In 1965 Elsie and Harry were persuaded to leave Admiral Grove for a house Ringo had bought them in Gateacre.

THE EMPRESS PUBLIC HOUSE, HIGH PARK STREET

Ringo Starr's 'local' was certainly that, just twenty yards from his front door in adjoining Admiral Grove. When, in 1970, Ringo released his first solo album *Sentimental Journey,* he immortalised The Empress by putting a photograph of it on the front cover.

ST SILAS PRIMARY SCHOOL, PENGWERN STREET

Ringo officially attended this school, a hundred yards from his home, between 1945 and 1950. In reality he spent very little time here. When he was six years old, he was admitted to the Royal Children's Hospital on Myrtle Street suffering from peritonitis. He underwent two operations, and stayed in hospital for twelve months. A classmate of Ringo was Ronald Wycherley, who was later destined to become Billy Fury, Liverpool's first rock star, and who later appeared with Ringo in the 1973 film *That'll Be The Day*.

**DINGLE VALE SECONDARY SCHOOL, DINGLE VALE
(NOW SHOREFIELDS COMPREHENSIVE SCHOOL)**

Probably due to his illness and resultant lack of schooling, Ringo was not allowed to take the eleven-plus examination. It was decided by his primary school teachers that he would be unable to pass it. Ringo therefore attended Dingle Vale Secondary School when he was eleven, the only Beatle not to have had a grammar school education. Again he was dogged by ill-health: at thirteen he was struck by pleurisy, and Ringo returned to the Children's Hospital. While he was there he joined a children's band and became interested in the drums. When Ringo went to Dingle Vale for a reference in 1955, he says that nobody could remember him. Strange then, that ten years later, the school was able to point out the very desk once occupied by their most famous ex-pupil.

ROSEBERY STREET, LIVERPOOL 8

The Quarrymen played here on 22 June 1957 during a street party to celebrate Liverpool's seven hundred years as a city. The charter was granted by King John in 1257. The gig is credited in most Beatles biographies as the band's first, but this is incorrect, since they had been playing at St Peter's Church Hall in Woolton for quite some time. They played an afternoon and evening set, which had to be abandoned after some local youths started to threaten Lennon. They retreated into a house belonging to a friend of drummer Colin Hanton, and the police were called. Later, they made their escape to the bus stop with a police escort.

THE PAVILION, LODGE LANE, LIVERPOOL 8

John Lennon's influences were of course not confined to American rock 'n roll. Like most British kids growing up in the first half of the twentieth century, he was receptive to music hall. Many of the finest exponents were born in Liverpool, including Tommy Handley, Arthur Askey, Wilson (of Wilson, Kepple and Betty) and Robb Wilton. The Pavilion was the city's last bastion of that curious phenomenon. John would either go alone, or persuade other art students to accompany him to the 7.00 pm or 9.00 pm show at the 'Pivvy'. Later, the grand old music hall held 'Beat Shows', and The Beatles played on the hallowed stage, once only, on 2 April 1962. The support act was the Royal Waterford Show Band from Ireland. Amazingly the 'Pivvy' still stands, and is currently the Pivvy Snooker Club.

LIVERPOOL GARDEN FESTIVAL SITE, CAST IRON SHORE

Once upon a time, Liverpool had its own beach, officially called Dingle shore, but known to all as the Cast Iron Shore, or Cassie. In the thirties and forties, children spent much of their summer holidays on the Cassie, collecting firewood, catching crabs in the rock pools and playing in the nearby woods or caves. The only known film footage available is in the 1958 production *Dangerous Youth* starring Liverpudlian Frankie Vaughan. Lennon made reference to the Cassie in the 1968 song *Glass Onion*. In the early eighties, when the city fathers were planning the 1984 Liverpool Garden Festival, the Cast Iron Shore was obliterated in the name of progress. The photograph was taken at the height of that summer, and the Cassie now lies beneath the Yellow Submarine.

9, NEWCASTLE ROAD

Formerly the home of the family of Mimi and Julia, John Lennon was brought here from Oxford Street Maternity Hospital some time in October 1940. His mother Julia Lennon was living with her parents, as her husband, John's father Freddie Lennon, was at sea with the Merchant Navy. Julia often left baby John in his cot in a dark room while she went out. This practice, it has been suggested, traumatised her son, leaving him with a life-long fear of the dark. In fact it is possible that the unconventional upbringing he received in his first five years of life at Newcastle Road shaped many of the less attractive sides of his complex character. His aunt, Julia's sister Mimi, was sufficiently disturbed by what she saw to offer to take John to her family home in wealthy Menlove Avenue. Julia needed little persuasion. After all, she was a young attractive woman, all but estranged from her husband. She wanted her freedom and Mimi wanted John. It was a perfect solution for both of them, so some time in 1945 John left Newcastle Road for what was to become a happier and more secure life at 251 Menlove Avenue.

MOSSPITS LANE PRIMARY SCHOOL, MOSSPITS LANE

It has only been discovered recently that John Lennon was once a pupil here. The school found his forty-five-year-old records a few years ago. It seems he was enrolled here in September 1945, only to be transferred to Dovedale six months later, in March 1946, on the instructions of his Aunt Mimi. Exactly whey she did this has never been fully explained, but it was not an uncommon practice, if a parent or guardian wished to do so. Albert Goldman claims in his book *The Lives of John Lennon* that John was expelled from Mosspits for 'disruptive behaviour'.

THE ABBEY CINEMA, CHURCH ROAD NORTH

This was John Lennon's local cinema. Although there was one in Woolton village, this was his favourite and was mentioned in the original lyrics of *In My Life*. It was here, with his girlfriends or Pete Shotton, that he saw many of his favourite films, like *Heaven Fell That Night* starring Brigitte Bardot, and *The Wild Ones* with Marlon Brando. He probably did not see an awful lot of what was on the screen, as he was almost blind without his glasses, which he was loath to wear at any time, especially in public. In 1965, the cinema was one of the first to present Cinerama, a strange, slightly disturbing experience involving three linked giant screens and very loud surround-sound. Sadly, however, it went the way of many British cinemas and became a supermarket in the eighties.

12, ARNOLD GROVE

George Harrison, the fourth child of Louise and Harold Harrison, was born in this red terraced house on 25 February 1943. Their rent was ten shillings a week, and they stayed here until moving to the new council estate at Speke in 1950. George still has affection for his birthplace. A few years ago he took his wife Olivia to see it. In his book *I Me Mine* his main recollection of the house was how cold it could be in the winter, with ice forming on the inside of the tiny windows, and the difficulty he had in getting out of bed on frosty mornings.

THE PENNY LANE ROUNDABOUT, SMITHDOWN PLACE

Penny Lane is obviously an important Beatles landmark, but it is often a disappointment to the traveller. In fact none of the places mentioned in the song is in Penny Lane. They are clustered around the roundabout, which is in Smithdown Place, at the junction of Church Road, Heathfield Road, Smithdown Road and Allerton Road. In the middle is a small, low, one-storey building which, in the fifties and sixties, was a bus terminus, waiting-room and public convenience. Opposite, towards Church Road, will be found the barber, now called Slavin, although The Beatles knew it as Bioletti's. Towards Allerton Road is 'the banker on the corner' (TSB plc). The single-storey building next to TSB was once an Albert Marrion studio. Albert took the very first publicity photographs of The Beatles in 1961. Looking across to St Barnabas Church, Penny Lane is to the right, and apart from the fact that it runs past Dovedale Towers to Dovedale School, it is really of little interest.

SAINT BARNABAS CHURCH, ELM HALL DRIVE

For a short time Paul McCartney was a member of the choir in this Anglican church. From here he made application to audition for the cathedral choir in 1953. On 29 May 1982, Peter Michael McCartney married Rowena Horne, his second wife, at Saint Barnabas. Paul was best man, and crowds of fans waited outside patiently for a glimpse of the McCartney brothers.

SAINT BARNABAS CHURCH HALL, PENNY LANE (NOW DOVEDALE TOWERS)
The Quarrymen played at this large hall several times in 1957 and 1958. No actual dates were recorded, but this was a major venue for skiffle dances and contests. In 1979, when Dick Clark's film crew arrived in Penny Lane for location filming for his TV movie *The Birth of The Beatles*, it was arranged to use the ballroom as the location for the Blue Angel/Larry Parnes audition of 1960.

DOVEDALE ROAD PRIMARY SCHOOL, DOVEDALE ROAD

John Lennon and George Harrison were both pupils here. John, the elder, between 1945 and 1951, and George, three years younger, between 1948 and 1950. Because of their age difference they probably never met. It was here that John would have learned two songs beloved of generations of Liverpool schoolchildren. The first was *Yellow Matter Custard,* from which he later used the first line in the 1967 song *I Am The Walrus.* The second was *Remember, Remember,* a celebration of Guy Fawkes Night. He used the first two lines on his 1970 solo song *Remember*.

HOLYOAKE HALL, SMITHDOWN ROAD

This was built by the Co-operative Society at the turn of the century. The ballroom is situated on the first floor of the building, which now houses the Royal British Legion, Wavertree Branch. Tea dances in the thirties: jive dances in the forties: skiffle and rock 'n roll in the fifties: the hall has hosted them all. The place is huge and has hardly changed in five decades. Although we only have one recorded gig for The Beatles here, 15 July 1961, they did compete in several skiffle contests at the Holyoake in 1957 and 1958. On 16 November 1990, a 'Holyoake Reunion' was held, with proceeds going to local charities. Appearing were Karl Terry and The Cruisers, The Undertakers, Johnny Guitar and The Hurricanes, and the all-encompassing Merseycats, of which Paul McCartney is an honorary member. (He has not appeared with them to date).

THE OLD DUTCH CAFE, 316, SMITHDOWN ROAD

In the late fifties and early sixties The Old Dutch Cafe was unusual because it stayed open all night. It catered for taxi drivers, strays on their way home from clubland, and rock bands looking for something to eat at 3.00am or 4.00am. The Beatles were friendly with the owner and often called here for bacon sandwiches after a gig, since it was situated on the main road into town and was less than twenty minutes from each of their homes. 'The Dutchy' was mentioned in Lennon's original lyrics (un-recorded) to *In My Life*. The cafe closed in the early seventies and has housed various businesses since then.

SEFTON GENERAL HOSPITAL, SMITHDOWN ROAD

On 15 July 1958, after visiting her sister Mimi Smith on Menlove Avenue, Julia Lennon was knocked down by a car at the junction of Beaconsfield Road, Menlove Avenue and Yew Tree Road. The attending ambulance quickly took her to Sefton General Hospital where she died soon afterwards. Nearly five years later, John's first son, named Julian after his grandmother, was born here. John's visits to wife Cynthia in the maternity ward had nurses, doctors and patients ogling the now famous Beatle. Until recently it was thought by some fans that John himself had been born at Sefton. This mistaken belief had its origins in an early interview given by Mimi, in which she said that on hearing the telephoned news of John's birth, she ran all the way to the hospital. From Newcastle Road to Sefton General is about a mile, whereas the distance to Oxford Street is nearer four. It now seems more likely that she ran for a taxi, since official papers have now confirmed Oxford Street as his birthplace.

37, AIGBURTH DRIVE, OFF ULLET ROAD, SEFTON PARK
Stuart Sutcliffe's mother, Millie, had a flat here at the time of her son's death in Hamburg on 10 April 1962. Born in Edinburgh, Scotland, on 2 June 1940, Stuart Ferguson Victor Sutcliffe had one sister, Pauline. On his application for a visa for the Hamburg trip in 1960, he gave his address as 53, Ullet Road, which is close by. Whether this was Stuart's own flat or a previous family home is uncertain. Aigburth Drive overlooks Sefton Park, where Alfred and Julia Lennon met one Sunday afternoon in 1928.

197, QUEENS DRIVE, CHILDWALL

This five-bedroomed house in one of Liverpool's most attractive suburbs was Brian Epstein's family home, on and off, for nearly thirty years. He shared it with his mother and father, Malka (Queenie) and Harry, and two live-in staff: a general help and a nanny for the boys. On the morning of Paul McCartney's twenty-first birthday, 18 June 1963, Brian hosted a cocktail party in his honour. When the Epsteins left 197, Queens Drive in the sixties, the house became the residence of the Dean of Liverpool.

GRAHAM SPENCER STUDIO, QUEENS DRIVE, CHILDWALL FIVEWAYS

Now sadly no longer with us, Graham took many of the best photographs of the early Beatles. One day in 1963, Brian Epstein, who lived three hundred yards away, had an idea to photograph together his three most successful groups: The Beatles: Gerry and The Pacemakers: Billy J. Kramer and The Dakotas. Graham was commissioned and the resulting photograph was taken in the car park of the Fiveways public house opposite, with Graham's studio in the background.

THE FOUR SEASONS (ENTRANCE TO CALDERSTONES PARK), HARTHILL ROAD
Directly opposite Quarry Bank, this is just one of several entrances to John's favourite park, Calderstones. He would be able to cycle nearly all the way home to 'Mendips' by riding through some of its ninety-four beautiful acres. He loved the park so much that, when he was looking for a new house in 1970, he bought Tittenhurst Park in Ascot because it reminded him of Calderstones. Because it was close to Quarry Bank, the young Lennon used the Four Seasons as a pre-school meeting place. It was his first stage. Standing on the low wall, he would harangue and amuse his fellow pupils before the academic day began.

QUARRY BANK GRAMMAR SCHOOL, HARTHILL ROAD
(NOW CALDER COMPREHENSIVE)

John Lennon entered the 'Eton of the Labour Party', Quarry Bank Grammar School, in September 1952. He had achieved it by passing the eleven-plus examination the previous June at Dovedale Road Juniors. From day one he fought the school's traditional values and teaching systems and soon gained a reputation as a waster and a rebel. He spent the next five years hating every minute of it, and, as is often the case, the following twenty-odd years fondly remembering his days there. As a result of government policy in the late sixties, the school changed from a boys-only grammar school to Calder Comprehensive. In John's day it was split into five houses: Childwall: Allerton: Woolton: Wavertree: Aigburth. He belonged to Woolton House, and contributed little or nothing to its sporting or academic effort.

QUARRY BANK GRAMMAR SCHOOL, HARTHILL ROAD (cont.)

The staff, including the headmaster Mr Pobjoy, recognised his wayward talent for art and wordplay, and for most of the five years he spent here, he was tolerated rather than encouraged. In later years he raged, 'If I'm a genius, why didn't they spot it when I was at school?' It could be that John did not exhibit anything worthy of encouragement at Quarry Bank, or it could be, as Oscar Wilde once remarked, 'Genius is seldom recognised by the mediocre.' In July 1957, he left the school as he had found it. Despite his strenuous efforts, its traditional values were still intact and he failed all four of the GCE 'O'-level examinations he had taken. Years later, as a famous Beatle, he told sycophantic pressmen, 'Look at me now. I've travelled all over the world and done these interesting things. I'm so well off and there are people who taught me at Quarry Bank who are *still* there.' In 1965 Mr Pobjoy met Aunt Mimi one day in Woolton village. The kindly headmaster enquired about John. 'Oh! he's fine,' replied Mimi, 'and do you know, he has his school photograph above his bed in his new house.' A decade later, during one of his regular transatlantic telephone calls to her Dorset home, John casually asked if she still had his old school tie, and if so, could she mail it to him. She did, and John took to wearing it about the streets of New York.

20, FORTHLIN ROAD

This neat, ex-council property was the last Liverpool home of Paul McCartney. Until a few years ago one could still see the black mountain ash that Jim McCartney had planted under Paul's bedroom window. His room was the smallest of three, and was situated above the front door. The McCartneys moved here from 12, Ardwick Road, Speke in 1955. It was Paul's seventh home, and for Beatles fans by far the most important.

20, FORTHLIN ROAD (cont.)

After Mary died of cancer in 1956, Jim was left to bring up Paul and Michael on his own. Because he was out all day at the Cotton Exchange, it became an ideal place for John and Paul to practise. Many of The Beatles finest songs were written around Jim's piano in the small front parlour. *The One After 909: I Saw Her Standing There: Love Me Do: When I'm Sixty-four:* are some of the more well-known songs finished at Forthlin. The output of the 'Nurk Twins' was torrential, and they filled dozens of exercise books with song lyrics and ideas, including a play about a Christ-like figure who spent all his life in one room. Early in 1963, Paul woke Mike late one night to announce that he had a very special surprise for him. Mike rubbed the sleep from his eyes and found the beautiful red-haired actress Jane Asher standing before him. In time-honoured northern tradition, Paul had brought her home to meet the family. One evening in spring 1964, the McCartneys left Forthlin Road nervously and under the cover of darkness. The house had become too well-known and privacy had been sacrificed for Paul's fame. The McCartneys, with furniture van following, drove to Heswall on the Wirral, geographically twenty-six miles away, but socially several light-years from Forthlin Road. In the early eighties, Paul visited his old home. Comfortably ensconced in his air-conditioned Mercedes, he parked outside number 20. A young local lad approached the car, unaware of the identity of the driver. 'Yeh,' the lad announced, with all the vanity of the story-teller, 'it's *his* house.' Paul nodded his thanks, smiled and drove away. It could have been Mike or him, thirty years earlier.

ALLERTON GOLF COURSE, MENLOVE AVENUE

It takes twenty minutes to walk from Paul's house in Forthlin Road to John's in Menlove Avenue, if your route is directly across Allerton golf course. The two friends often made the short journey to and fro. More than once, Paul, who would have used the Allerton Road entrance opposite Wheatcroft Avenue, lost in song, guitar strung across his chest, was disturbed by someone hurrying home from the other direction. He would quickly swing his guitar on his back, and try to hide his embarrassment by sheepishly whistling some non-existent melody. The 150-acre course was opened in 1924, a gift to the city from a merchant family, the Fletchers. Near the house at the centre of the course is a forty-foot high sandstone obelisk. Its four sides are aligned to the points of the compass, and it is exactly five miles from the city centre. Who built it, and for what reason remains a mystery.

THE COTTAGE,
120a, ALLERTON ROAD

This was originally the dairy farm owned by the family of Mimi's husband, George Smith. It later became home for Mimi's youngest sister Harriet. When Julia died, John's two half-sisters, Julia and Jaqueline, came to live here. John often visited his aunt and sisters, and after his marriage they went regularly to baby-sit for Julian. The house remained in family ownership until 1968, when John bought Harriet another house in Woolton. During John's sentimental journey to Liverpool with Yoko in 1970, they had dinner in Woolton with Harriet, who was shocked by his macrobiotic diet, but impressed by the couple's obvious closeness.

'MENDIPS', 251, MENLOVE AVENUE

Once it had been decided between John's mother, Julia, and Mimi, his aunt, that Mimi should assume responsibility for John's upbringing, he was moved here some time in 1945 from 9, Newcastle Road. The black and white pre-war villa became his home for almost the next twenty years, before the pressure of fame necessitated a move. John then went to London and Mimi moved to a detached bungalow he had bought for her in Poole, Dorset.

'MENDIPS', 251, MENLOVE AVENUE (cont.)

John's bedroom was directly above the front door, which was, and still is, housed in a porch of glass and brick. It was in this tiny porch, in 1956 and 1957, that John practised continuously on his acoustic guitar. Three years later, John returned to Mendips after the band's first trip to Hamburg. After initial success, this trip had ended in disaster, the German police withdrawing their work permits. A delighted Mimi paid off the taxi, and offered her immortal advice to the tired, angry and incredibly skinny musician, 'A guitar's all right John, but you'll never make a living out of it.' Suitably chastened, Lennon retreated to his bedroom, hardly venturing out for nearly a fortnight, until George and Paul called. They persuaded him to rejoin the band for the now-legendary gig at Litherland Town Hall on 27 December 1960. It was at Mendips that Brian Epstein stilled fears of The Beatles' signing with him in 1962. Reassuringly, he told Mimi, 'I promise you Mrs Smith, John will never suffer. The others don't matter.' Mimi loved John, and John, despite his frequent rebellions, like going from time to time to live with Julia in Blomfield Road, loved Mimi. Even when he was touring the world, she would hop on the number 5 bus to Penny Lane, buy half a dozen of his favourite plastic combs from Woolworths, and promptly post them off to him, care of some exotic foreign address. A week before his death in December 1980, John phoned her with another request for something he needed from England. At the foot of his bed in the Dakota apartment complex was a sailor's simple wooden trunk. It was full of mementos, photographs and his Quarry Bank tie, and was labelled with one word - LIVERPOOL.

STRAWBERRY FIELD CHILDREN'S HOME, BEACONSFIELD ROAD

Here was one of the many children's homes run by the Salvation Army. The annual summer fete continues to this day. John visited the fetes and played in the large wooded grounds. By nipping out of his back garden in Menlove Avenue and crossing Vale Road, he could enter Strawberry Field by a rear entrance which no longer exists. In 1967, The Beatles had a number 1 hit with their double-A-sided single *Penny Lane/Strawberry Fields Forever,* the promotion film for which is now considered to be the first pop video. John wrote *Strawberry Fields Forever* and Paul wrote *Penny Lane.* The original building has since been demolished and replaced; only the red wrought-iron gate remains from the fifties. In 1984, Yoko and Sean visited the children of Strawberry Field, and they have continued to support them financially.

REYNOLDS PARK, CHURCH ROAD, WOOLTON VILLAGE

John Lennon's second-favourite Liverpool park was a place of play for the child gang-leader, and later an oasis of calm for concentrating his thoughts as an adolescent. It was here, on 15 July 1958, that John's first real girlfriend, Barbara Baker, tried to console the grieving art student after his mother had just died in Sefton General Hospital. The fourteen acres were given to the city by Sir James Reynolds in 1929, and it is certainly a quiet, charming place to visit.

ST PETER'S CHURCH, CHURCH ROAD

This Victorian Church of England was John Lennon's local church in the forties and fifties. At different stages of his growth he belonged to the Sunday school, the choir and the youth club. On the day John and Paul first met, 6 July 1957, The Quarrymen had been contracted to play twice. The first set was at 4.15pm, in the field behind the church, as part of the annual fete. The second was at 5.45pm in the church hall opposite. During the afternoon set John spotted Mimi heading straight for him and changed the lyrics accordingly, 'Uh oh here comes Mimi heading straight for me, I'm goin' down to the penitentiary.' Other attractions at the 1957 fete, which is still held annually, were the Liverpool Police Dogs Display, and the crowning of the Rose Queen, Miss Sally Wright.

ST. PETER'S CHURCH HALL, CHURCH ROAD

This was the first venue The Quarrymen ever played. They played here regularly on Saturday nights for the church's youth club dances. On 6 July 1957, after another Quarrymen gig, sixteen-year-old John Lennon was introduced to fifteen-year-old Paul McCartney by a mutual friend and occasional Quarryman Ivan Vaughan. Earlier, watching from the wings, Paul had noticed John's awkward banjo chords, taught to him by Julia, and lost no time demonstrating to the band his knowledge of the guitar by playing straight through Eddie Cochran's *Twenty Flight Rock* and Little Richard's *Long Tall Sally*. After a couple of weeks of indecision, Lennon asked his best friend Pete Shotton to contact Paul with an invitation to join the band. According to McCartney, it took him a full minute to think about it before accepting. Paul's debut with The Quarrymen was probably at a youth club dance in the church hall, some time in late August 1957. The hall and its interior have remained mostly unchanged in the last thirty-five years.

WOOLTON SWIMMING BATHS, ALLERTON ROAD, WOOLTON VILLAGE
Woolton swimming baths are situated at the corner of Quarry Street and Allerton Road, and just a few hundred yards from John's sisters' home at 120a, Allerton Road. John visited the baths regularly as a boy and as a teenager. He was even a member of the Woolton Swimming Club at one point. The remains of the famous Woolton Quarry can still be seen half-way up Quarry Street. It was from the quarry that The Quarrymen got their name, not Quarry Bank Grammar School, as is generally believed.

WOOLTON VILLAGE CLUB, ALLERTON ROAD

This Victorian building, situated in the heart of the village, was the scene of several Quarrymen gigs, the last-recorded date being 24 January 1959. The club has hardly changed since those days.

1, BLOMFIELD ROAD, SPRINGWOOD

After John was safely ensconced in 'Mendips' with Mimi, Julia was free to find her own life. She eventually met waiter Bobby Dykins, and moved into his home here on the Springwood council estate. Bobby and Julia had two daughters, Julia and Jaqueline, and John was a frequent visitor and overnight guest when Mimi's nagging became too much. John and Paul rehearsed in the bathroom, since the acoustics sounded to them like a recording studio. Julia loved rock 'n roll so much that she even named the cat 'Elvis'. On the night Julia was killed, John was staying at Blomfield Road: in fact he opened the door to the police. He went to Sefton General with Dykins to identify the body. Bobby never recovered from Julia's death and moved from Blomfield Road soon afterwards. Since the fifties, the house has changed a lot for the better, and the present owner recently won a 'best-kept garden' competition.

GARSTON BATHS, SPEKE ROAD

All four Beatles are fair swimmers, and at least three of them, John, Paul and George, visited Garston baths on Saturday mornings in the fifties. After dark the pool was boarded over, and dances were held which were very dangerous. There were rival gangs like 'The Tigers' and 'The Tank' doing battle, and the place became known as 'The Blood Baths'. The police rarely intervened, leaving the dozen-or-so bouncers to keep the peace. This was achieved by wielding wooden baseball bats. The Quarrymen probably played at more than one of these 'hops' in the late fifties.

THE WILSON HALL, SPEKE ROAD

This was one of two clubs run by Charlie McBain, the first man to pay The Quarrymen. They played here dozens of times during 1957 and 1958. It was here that George Harrison made his debut with the band after meeting them a month or so previously in the Morgue, an illegal club in Old Swan. George had played a flawless version of *Raunchy* in a backroom. This resulted in the manager of The Quarrymen, Nigel Whalley, turning to drummer Colin Hanton and saying, 'That's it. George is in. Eric Griffiths is out.' During the sixties the building housed 'Lennons' supermarket (no relation) and it now belongs to Woolton Carpets.

GARSTON BOTTLE WORKS, WINDOW LANE

A tragi-comic scenario involving John, Paul, George, Stuart and drummer Tommy Moore, took place here in June 1960. On the insistence of his girlfriend, Moore had quit the band, shortly after the Johnny Gentle tour, in favour of a steady job driving a fork-lift truck on the night shift here at Garston Bottle Works. On the way to The Grosvenor Ballroom in Wallasey, The Silver Beatles and manager Allan Williams stopped off here to try to persuade Tommy to rejoin the band. Poor old Tommy stuck to his guns, and despite being subjected to a torrent of abuse from the lads, his only reply was a slightly sad, 'See ya boys.' Nine years later, during a heated Beatles rehearsal, Lennon said to Paul, within hearing of Ringo, 'Tommy Moore was the best bloody drummer we ever had.' The works closed down several years ago.

72, WESTERN AVENUE

Paul's mum, Mary Patricia McCartney, had been working as a midwife in Speke for some time before the family secured this house on the large council estate in 1947. The McCartneys stayed here for nearly six years before moving to Ardwick Road in 1953. Nearly thirty years later, the then owner, while tidying the tiny loft, found a Rupert Bear annual inscribed with the legend: 'This book belongs to Paul and Michael McCartney, 72 Western Avenue, Speke'. Paul quickly bought it back and started a new craze of Rupert-mania.

12, ARDWICK ROAD

This was the sixth home of James, Mary, Paul and Michael. Because Mary was a midwife, she had influence with the council, and was able to secure this new house for the family in 1953. The McCartneys moved in shortly after Paul's eleventh birthday and his final year at Joseph Williams School in Gateacre. Paul passed the eleven-plus easily and was awarded a place at his first choice school, the one hundred-year-old Liverpool Institute. For the first two years he would have had to commute the twenty-mile round trip daily. In 1955, Mary used her influence again, and the family was on the move for the last time to 20, Forthlin Road in nearby Allerton.

STOCKTON WOOD JUNIOR SCHOOL, STOCKTON WOOD DRIVE
Paul McCartney attended this school from 1947. Some time in the early fifties the school became overcrowded, and Paul was transferred to Joseph Williams, quite a distance away in Netherley.

25, UPTON GREEN

The Harrison family moved into Upton Green some time in 1950 and stayed for nearly twelve years. Mrs Harrison was the only Beatle parent to give active encouragement to the band, and they practised in this tiny terraced house many times. On 20 December 1958, The Quarrymen played at the wedding reception of George's brother, Harry, at Upton Green.

JOSEPH WILLIAMS PRIMARY SCHOOL, NAYLORSFIELD ROAD, BELLE VALE
This was Paul's last and main primary school, where he sat and passed the eleven-plus examination in 1953. His brother Michael also attended Joseph Williams, and later followed Paul to the Liverpool Institute.

THE ROYAL BRITISH LEGION (SPEKE), CONLEACH ROAD

Some time in late 1957, fourteen-year-old George Harrison announced to his mother Louise that he had an audition at the local British Legion. When she pointed out that he did not have a group, he told her not to worry, he would get one. The group he had hurriedly assembled, calling themselves The Rebels, consisted of George, his brother Peter, best friend Arthur Kelly (now a well-known actor from *Brookside, Bergerac, etc.*) and two others. The Rebels eventually played the entire Saturday night, because no other artists had arrived. They were paid ten shillings each. The Rebels did not last long, and George did not belong to any other band until he joined The Quarrymen in 1958. In 1988, George sent £3500 to the Speke Boys Club, which was in danger of closure.

174, MACKETS LANE, HUNTS CROSS, NEAR SPEKE

Here is George Harrison's last home in Liverpool, where the family lived for only eighteen months, after moving in during 1962. Once The Beatles became nationally famous, life for the Harrisons was impossible, so George bought a new home for the family in Warrington and moved to London himself, to share a flat with Ringo. Trudy and Robert Goodwin, who moved in immediately after the Harrisons, say that George's room had three yellow walls, one bright scarlet and a black ceiling. The Goodwins sold the ex- council property in 1987 for £28,000. Incidentally, George's local shop at Mackets Lane was 'Tushingham's', owned and run by the parents of film star Rita Tushingham.

OLD TERMINAL BUILDING, LIVERPOOL AIRPORT, SPEKE ROAD

The Beatles used this fifty-five-year-old airstrip dozens of times. The terminal is now disused, abandoned in the eighties for a new steel and glass construction, two miles south, behind Speke Hall (or as Lennon called it, 'Talke Hall'). Back in the early sixties, British Eagle's turbo-prop Viscounts held the Liverpool-London contract, and on 10 July 1964, The Beatles returned home for a civic reception and the northern premiere of *A Hard Day's Night*. The viewing gallery, where George and Paul had watched the 'airies' land as children, was full of ecstatic fans cheering, screaming and waving banners. Paul continues to use the airport. For his return-home concert, in June 1990, the whole family flew in aboard his chartered Lear Jet.

M.P.T.E SOCIAL CLUB, FINCH LANE

George Harrison's father, Harold, was a bus driver and an official for his union. Here at Finch Lane was the company's social club and sports grounds. Unfortunately, the club has now been demolished. Both Harold and Louise encouraged George's musical talents, and Harold used his influence on entertainment committees to find suitable gigs for The Quarrymen. It was at one such gig, in 1958, that The Quarrymen played two spots at the social club, as an audition for the manager of The Pavilion, Lodge Lane. The first half went well, and the crowd seemed to enjoy the mix of rock 'n roll and skiffle provided by the eager youngsters. However, they got drunk during the interval, and the second half was a disaster. John and Paul were giggling and laughing, and took the mickey out of George, whose mum and dad were in the audience. Drummer Colin Hanton was so annoyed about the missed opportunity that he quit the band after the gig. Coincidentally, the band which won the job at 'The Pivvie' was The Darktown Skiffle Group, which included a seventeen-year-old drummer named Richard Starkey.

HAMBLETON HALL, ST DAVID'S ROAD

Ten miles east of the city centre and typical of the small suburban dance halls that The Beatles were playing in 1961, they played here eleven times, from the first gig on 20 January 1961 to the last on 13 January 1962. It was at one of the later gigs that the group asked their growing army of followers to go out and buy the recently-released Polydor single *My Bonnie*, which they had recorded in Hamburg with Tony Sheridan in June 1961.

THE CASBAH CLUB,
8 HAYMANS GREEN,
WEST DERBY VILLAGE

In August 1959, a new club was opened in the quiet village suburb of West Derby. It was run solely for teenagers by the owner, Mrs Mona Best, and her eldest son Peter. Peter played the drums in his own band, The Blackjacks. A friend of Lennon, Ken Browne, introduced him to the Bests, and The Quarrymen were asked to play the opening night at the new club (named 'The Casbah', after Charles Boyer's hiding place in the 1938 film *Algiers*). Pete joined The Beatles on 17 August 1960, shortly before they embarked on their first trip to Hamburg. The Bests' large Victorian home became The Beatles' headquarters, and Mrs Best constantly helped and encouraged the band. Pete's popularity with the fans was legend, girls actually camping out on his front lawn. The Quarrymen/Silver Beatles/Beatles played the basement club at least two hundred times between 1959 and 1962, and it was here, not at NEMS Whitechapel, that they signed their contract with Brian Epstein on 24 January 1962.

KNOTTY ASH VILLAGE HALL, EAST PRESCOT ROAD, KNOTTY ASH

Knotty Ash, a tiny hamlet south of West Derby, is the home of Britain's most successful comedian, Ken Dodd. The Beatles played at the village hall six times, the first on 15 September 1961, and the last on 17 March 1962. They also worked with Ken on several occasions in the early sixties. On 15 October 1961, they appeared as support for him at Maghull's Albany Cinema, in a charity show. Two years later, they were on his BBC radio show, on 3 November 1963, after being interviewed with him on the same day for local TV's *People and Places*. During that interview, Ken said he too would like to be a pop star, but felt he needed the right name. Paul suggested Rock, whilst George dryly thought Sod was more suitable.

ALDER HEY CHILDREN'S HOSPITAL, EATON ROAD

The hospital has just celebrated its seventy-fifth birthday with a massive charity appeal. Paul has been involved with the fund-raising, part of the proceeds for his Kings Dock Concert in 1990 going to the appeal. He modestly explains his involvement by saying his mother Mary once worked here. In November 1990, he came in for some criticism when the video *All My Trials* was released. Some of the scenes had been filmed at Alder Hey, and because of the imagery, he was accused of 'making a vitriolic attack on the Tory government'. The McCartneys' close friend, writer Carla Lane, with whom Linda wrote an anti-vivisection song *The White Coated Man,* has a house nearby.

WALTON HOSPITAL, RICE LANE, WALTON

James Paul McCartney was born here on 18 June 1942. His mother, Mary Patricia, had once been a Sister in charge of the maternity ward, and when she returned to have her first baby, she was given five-star treatment. Ex-colleagues insisted that she stay in a private ward. Paul's dad Jim, an aircraft worker at Napier's by day and a fire warden at night, was not impressed on first seeing his son … 'He looked awful. I couldn't get over it. Horrible. He had one eye open, and he just squawked all the time. But the next day he looked more human and every day after that he got better and better.'

10, SUNBURY ROAD, ANFIELD

Some time in late June 1942, Jim and Mary McCartney brought their first son, James Paul, home to rented rooms in this small terraced house near the two football stadia of Liverpool FC and Everton FC. The McCartneys did not stay long in Sunbury Road. Once the bombing of Liverpool by the Luftwaffe started in earnest, the family moved to the comparatively safe district of Wallasey, on the Wirral.

LITHERLAND TOWN HALL, HATTON HILL ROAD, LITHERLAND

This imposing-looking building was the scene of some rough and raucous dances in the early sixties. The Beatles played their first gig here on their return from their first trip to Hamburg on 27 December 1960. Brian Kelly billed them as 'Direct from Germany', and most people who were there that night remember the difference in their performance. The previous four months in Hamburg's St Pauli nightclubs had turned them into a hard and hungry powerhouse. Another memorable night at the Town Hall was 19 October 1961, when, after finishing their own sets, The Beatles and Gerry and The Pacemakers joined forces as The Beatmakers. With Lennon on piano, the first 'rockestra' blasted their way through: *Whole Lotta Shakin': What'd I Say: Red Sails In The Sunset: and Hit The Road Jack.* Altogether the Beatles played here eight times, and their last gig was on 9 November 1961.

LATHOM HALL, LATHOM AVENUE, SEAFORTH

Introducing themselves as The Silver Beats, John, Paul, George and Stuart auditioned for promoter Brian Kelly during the interval at a Saturday night dance on 14 May 1960. They must have been good, because Kelly booked them for the following Saturday, 21 May. Unfortunately, they could not fulfil this engagement, the first advertised Beatle gig anywhere, as by then they had embarked on the hastily-arranged Scottish tour with Johnny Gentle. It is generally believed that it was during a fight with some local lads at Lathom Hall where Stuart Sutcliffe received a head injury which later developed into his fatal brain tumour. They went on to play this tough North End dance hall a further eight times, the last being on George's eighteenth birthday, 25 February 1961.

AINTREE INSTITUTE, LONGMOOR LANE, FAZAKERLY

Although it is situated six miles outside the city, The Beatles were very popular in Aintree. The Institute, a dance hall since the thirties, tried to book the band as often as they could for their regular dance nights. They worked here at least fifteen times, the first being on 1 March 1961 and the last on 27 January 1962.

THE WIRRAL

Merseyrail: *From any Liverpool station, any underground Wirral train, alight Birkenhead, Hamilton Square. Journey time 15 mins.*
Merseyferry: *From the Pier Head*
By road: *Queensway tunnel (toll).*

MAJESTIC BALLROOM, CONWAY STREET, BIRKENHEAD

The Beatles first played here on 28 June 1962. They went on to play a further sixteen gigs at the ballroom, including their last on 10 April 1963. It was at one of the latter gigs that Cilla Black, then known as Priscilla White, auditioned successfully for Brian Epstein, with backing from The Beatles.

Merseyrail: From any Liverpool station, any underground Hooton Line train, alight Bebington. Journey time 15 mins. Walk back up Old Chester Road, turn into Town Lane, walk to top. Walk 10 mins.
By road: Queensway tunnel (toll), A41, B5136.

VICTORIA HALL, VILLAGE ROAD, BEBINGTON

England is littered with parks, monuments and halls named after her longest-serving monarch, and The Beatles played this one, only once, on 14 August 1962. John Lennon may have been familiar with Bebington, as his Aunt Anne lived and still lives in nearby Rock Ferry. John and Julia visited her Victorian terraced house regularly, and John's favourite photograph of his mother was taken in the neat back garden. Some of Paul's large family also live in Bebington, and he has been known to take a glass of wine at The Traveller's Rest, situated at the top of Village Road.

Merseyrail: From any Liverpool station, any underground Hooton Line train, alight Port Sunlight.
Journey time 25 mins.
By road: Queensway tunnel (toll), A41.

HULME HALL, PORT SUNLIGHT

The Beatles only played here four times, but it was a very important venue in Beatles history.
The first occasion was on 7 July 1962 with Pete Best. When they returned five weeks later, on
18 August, they had a new man behind the drum kit, and it was at Hulme Hall that Ringo Starr
made his debut with the Beatles. Shortly before their last performance here, on 27 October 1962,
they were interviewed by local hospital radio. The tape of that interview was thought to have been
lost until it turned up on a free flexi-disc in Mark Lewishon's excellent 1987 book *The Beatles Live.*

Merseyrail: From any Liverpool station, underground Wrexham Line, change at Bidston, alight
               Heswall. Journey time 40 mins.
By road: Queensway tunnel (toll), A552, A551.

HESWALL JAZZ CLUB, BARNSTON WOMEN'S INSTITUTE, BARNSTON VILLAGE
Situated in the tiny village of Barnston, next to the church, the Women's Institute was used by
the Heswall Jazz Club in the fifties and sixties. On the first occasion The Beatles played here,
23 March 1962, Brian Epstein designed the poster. Making the most of very little, it boasted, 'An
All Star Bill - The Beatles, Merseybeat Poll Winners, Polydor Recording Artists, Prior to European
Tour.' The support act was The Pasadena Jazzmen, and tickets cost 7s 6d (£0.375). The band played
a further two engagements at the institute on 30 June and 25 September 1962.

*Merseyrail: From any Liverpool station, any underground New Brighton line tain. Alight Wallasey
Village. Journey time 20 mins.*
By road: Wallasey tunnel (toll).

92, BROADWAY AVENUE, WALLASEY

The McCartneys stayed here for a year, between 1942 and 1943. Paul's father, Jim, was 37 when
war broke out in 1939. He was not called up, partly because of his age, and also because he worked
in vital aircraft production at the Napier Aircraft Factory in Knowsley. In 1943, the McCartneys
were on the move again, this time back over the Mersey to Roach Avenue, Knowsley. Twelve months
later they moved once more, to 75, Sir Thomas White Gardens, Everton Valley, where they stayed
until relocating to Speke in 1947. Neither Roach Avenue nor Sir Thomas White Gardens is in
existence today.

Merseyrail: From any Liverpool station, any underground New Brighton line train, alight Wallasey Village, bus to Liscard village.
By road: Wallasey tunnel (toll), A551.

GROSVENOR BALLROOM, GROSVENOR STREET, LISCARD VILLAGE, WALLASEY
Another Beatles venue that has not changed since the fifties, the Grosvenor was probably the toughest on the Wirral. The group's first performance here was on 4 June 1960, sharing the bill with Gerry and The Pacemakers. Allan Williams, who booked them the gig, took £2.00 as agent's commission from the £10.00 they were paid. They played here several times, their set being interrupted more than once by local gangs fighting on the dance floor. Paul even had an amplifier stolen right before his eyes. He wisely decided not to challenge the thugs making off with his pride and joy. The Beatles' last gig at the 'brawl' room was on 15 September 1961.

Merseyrail: From any Liverpool station, any underground New Brighton line train, alight New Brighton. Journey time 25 mins.
By road: Wallasey tunnel (toll), A554.

CHELSEA REACH PUBLIC HOUSE, VICTORIA ROAD, NEW BRIGHTON
(NOW ROYALE CLUB)

This was McCartney's favourite pub in the early seventies. He could often be spotted enjoying a glass or two of wine in the trendy hostelry. In fact he liked it so much that he put it in his 1973 TV special *James Paul McCartney.* It has probably been a watering-hole since Victorian times, when the pier, and the Tivoli Gardens which were opposite, were used by hundreds of day-trippers and holiday-makers arriving by ferry from Liverpool.

Merseyrail: From any Liverpool station, any underground New Brighton line train, alight New
Brighton. Journey time 25 mins.
By road: Wallasey tunnel (toll), A554.

THE TOWER BALLROOM, NEW BRIGHTON

Just around the corner from the Chelsea Reach is the site of what used to be New Brighton Tower, which was even taller than that of Blackpool. Sadly, it burned down in mysterious circumstances in 1969, and all that can be seen today are the foundations. In the thirties, the grandfather of George Harrison was a commissionaire at the Tower's huge ballroom, which held 2000 people. The Beatles played the Tower dozens of times. After Epstein became their manager, he caused uproar one night by demanding that, instead of the band sharing the communal dressing room, they should have one of their own. For a time it looked like The Beatles would not play, but after a lot of threats, Epstein got his way. On another occasion Brian was roughed up after he had tried to stop two of the Tower's doormen from beating up a young lad.

Merseyrail: From any Liverpool station, any underground West Kirby Line train, alight West Kirby. Journey time 30 mins.
By road: Queensway tunnel (toll), A553.

THISTLE CAFE/MACDONNA HALL, SALISBURY AVENUE-BANKS ROAD CORNER
The first engagement secured for The Beatles by Brian Epstein was here in the small seaside town of West Kirby, on 10 February 1962. Brian persuaded the owner to advertise the gig as 'The Grand Opening Of The Beatle Club'. The Beatles were paid £18.00, and never returned. The Beatles' press officer, Derek Taylor, was born in West Kirby, and his first job was on the local paper *The Hoylake and West Kirby Advertiser.*

OUTLYING TOWNS

After Brian Epstein took on the management of The Beatles in December 1961, he began to secure them engagements outside Liverpool. In this section are six towns: Southport: Earlestown: St Helens: Widnes: Runcorn: Frodsham. All lie within a twenty-mile radius of the city. The band played them between 1962 and 1963. With the exception of two venues in Southport, all the buildings are still standing and in everyday use. They were important, as they provided a valuable testing ground for Brian's belief that The Beatles would have a national, and possibly international appeal.

Southport

THE FLORAL HALL, PROMENADE

The Beatles had only one appearance at the Floral Hall, on 20 November 1962, six days before recording *Please Please Me*.

THE LITTLE THEATRE, HOGHTON STREET

During the morning of 27 August 1963, The Beatles were filmed here before a live audience, for the BBC TV documentary *The Mersey Sound*. It was broadcast on John Lennon's twenty-third birthday, on 9 October 1963, in the London and North-west areas only. After the onset of Beatlemania (usually dated from the 13 October ATV broadcast *Sunday Night At The London Palladium)* the documentary was repeated nationwide, on 13 November 1963. Other venues in Southport played by The Beatles were: The Cambridge Hall, Lord Street: The Odeon Cinema, Lord Street: and The Kingsway Club on the promenade.

Rail: From Liverpool Lime Street station on the Manchester (Victoria) line. Journey time 30 mins.

THE TOWN HALL, EARLESTOWN, NEWTON-LE-WILLOWS

This one-hundred-year-old civic building regularly held dances until the mid-sixties. Directly opposite is the new police station, built on the site of the Pavilion which once presented legendary Lancashire comic and singer, George Formby. George Harrison is a long-standing member of Formby's appreciation society, and recently cited him as an influence on the humour of The Beatles. Towards the end of his life at the Dakota apartments, while working on new songs on his acoustic guitar, John would break into George's songs: *Mr Wu: Leaning On A Lamp-post:* and *When I'm Cleaning Windows*. The Beatles played the Town Hall on 30 November 1962, two days after recording *Please Please Me* at Abbey Road Studios. It was their one and only appearance in Earlestown.

Rail: *From Liverpool Lime Street station, Wigan North Western Line, alight St Helens, Shaw Street.*
        Journey time 30 mins.
By road: *A570*

PLAZA BALLROOM, DUKE STREET

Now Lowie's nightclub, the Plaza was part of the 'Whetstone Circuit', which controlled sixteen other venues in the north-west of England. Brian was therefore eager for The Beatles to do well here, and for the first gig he issued one of his well-known memos, reminding the band to arrive on time, and to be careful with their dress and programme continuity. A total of five performances was given here, usually of one hour's duration. The first, on 25 June 1962, was just three weeks after the EMI audition. The last was on 4 March 1963, the day before recording their first 'official' number one, *From Me To You.*

Rail: *From Liverpool Lime Street or Central (underground) stations, alight Widnes (Farnworth).*
By road: *A562, A5080 or B5178*

THE QUEENS HALL, VICTORIA ROAD

A total of six performances was given here, four of them organised by Brian Epstein's NEMS. The first was on 3 September 1962, when The Beatles had spent the day rehearsing at the Cavern Club in preparation for their first Parlophone recording session the next day. George Harrison was sporting a black eye which he had received from a disgruntled fan at the Cavern the night before. Feelings had still been running high over the sacking of drummer Pete Best. A month later, on 22 October, The Beatles were supported at the Queens Hall by Pete's new band, Lee Curtis and The All Stars. None of The Beatles spoke to Pete. Their last performance here was on 18 February 1963, just three days before New Musical Express showed *Please Please Me* at number one.

Rail: *From Liverpool Lime Street station. Journey time 15 mins.*
By road: *A561, A562*

LA SCALA, HIGH STREET

On 16 October 1962, The Beatles fulfilled the first of two engagements at this art deco ballroom, fifteen miles south of Liverpool. It was, coincidentally, the night before their first ever TV appearance, for local station Granada, on *People and Places*. Their second and last appearance at La Scala was on 11 December 1962, a week before leaving for their last residency at The Star Club in Hamburg. The ballroom has since become a bingo hall, but its exterior has hardly changed in fifty years, and the BBC recently used it in a TV film, set in the Liverpool of the 1930s.

Rail: From Liverpool Lime Street station, underground, change at Hooton. Journey time 35 mins.

MERSEYVIEW COUNTRY CLUB, OVERTON HILLS

Twenty miles from Liverpool and set in Cheshire, one of the richest counties in England; the view from behind the club, over the Mersey is breathtaking. The Merseyview is still very much in business, having had The Crickets play here in March 1991. The Beatles played here on 20 April 1963, two days after playing at the Royal Albert Hall in a performance which had been broadcast live by the BBC Light programme, for *Swing Sound '63*. One night in May 1974, while working on Mike McCartney's solo album *McGear* at Stockport's Strawberry Studios, the car being used by Paul, Mike and Linda broke down on the M56 motorway at Frodsham. Mike headed across the fields and telephoned the breakdown service, informing them that he was Mike McGear of The Scaffold. By the time the recovery vehicle arrived, Mike's message had become so jumbled that the mechanic announced brightly, 'Are you the party from McGear Scaffolding?'

DAY TRIPPER

Here are two tours which take in the more well-known Beatles sights. The city tour can be accomplished on foot in a couple of hours. The suburban tour takes a little longer, and will need the use of Merseybus.

For greater detail of each location, refer to the main text.

THE CITY CENTRE

Begin in Castle Street, at Liverpool Town Hall, scene of The Beatles civic reception on 10 July 1964. From here, walk towards the Victoria Monument, but turn left into Cook Street. At the next junction turn right into South John Street, and almost immediately opposite is Mathew Street. This is the Beatles Centre of the town, with The Cavern Walks Shopping Centre, Abbey Road Pub, The New Cavern, Arthur Dooley's 1974 sculpture, The John Lennon Club, and towards the bottom, The Beatles Shop and The Grapes public house. Turn left into Stanley street, and on the far side of the road is the Eleanor Rigby statue (1982) by Tommy Steele. Back across the road is Hessy's Music Shop, where The Beatles bought their first guitars.

A few yards on is the junction with Whitechapel, where immediately opposite is Rushworth's Music Store. Turn right, and near the end of Whitechapel (at its junction with Church Street) is Rumbelows. This was once the headquarters of Brian Epstein's NEMS.

Turn left and take a brisk walk up Church Street towards Central Station and next door to it is The Lyceum, which used to be a cafe frequented by The Beatles. Next to The Lyceum is Bold Street, where The Odd Spot Club used to be at number 89. Return along Bold Street and into Slater Street on the left. At number 23 is The Jacaranda Club, an old Silver Beatles headquarters from around 1960.

Retrace the route to take a right turn into Seel Street. Near the top, at number 108, is The Blue Angel Club, where in May 1960 The Silver Beatles auditioned for Billy Fury. Continue and turn right into Berry Street, cross the road and turn into Upper Duke Street. On the left will be Rodney Street, where Brian Epstein was born in 1935 in a private clinic. On the right is the city's Anglican Cathedral, where Paul McCartney unsuccessfully auditioned for the choir in 1954.

The next major street on the left is Hope Street. Turn into it, and almost immediately on the left is Mount Street. The first building to be seen is the Liverpool College of Art, which John attended from 1957 to 1960. Almost adjoining is the Liverpool Institute where Paul and George were educated. Return to Hope Street, turn left and the next street along is Rice Street. Here is to be found Ye

Cracke Public House, where the friendship between John and Stuart was cemented, and John and Cynthia fell in love.

Again return to Hope Street, turn left, and almost facing is the Royal Philharmonic Hall, where, at an Institute Prize Day in 1955, Paul took a prize for an essay he had written. Continue across the busy junction of Hardman Street, and on the left is The Philharmonic Dining Rooms, a Victorian pub where The Beatles enjoyed a pint or two. Further up, and at the end of Hope Street, with the Catholic Cathedral ahead, is The Everyman Theatre, which premiered the two Beatles subject plays, *John, Paul, George, Ringo and Bert* in 1974 and *Lennon* in 1982.

At the end of Hope Street, turn right into Arrad Street. This is the entrance to Oxford Street Maternity Hospital, where John Winston Lennon was born on 9 October 1940.

From Oxford Street, take any bus back to the Pier Head and The Beatles Story at the Albert Dock.

PENNY LANE - STRAWBERRY FIELD - WOOLTON VILLAGE - SPEKE

This tour can be done in four or five hours, but ideally allow a day for a more leisurely pace. At the Pier Head or Roe Street, opposite the Royal Court Theatre, where Paul played in November 1979, take the number 5 or 86 bus to Penny Lane. The route passes the Royal Children's Hospital on Myrtle Street, where Ringo was several times a patient as a child, and Sefton General Hospital, where Julia died and Julian was born. Further along Smithdown Road, within a few hundred yards of each other, are the Old Dutch Cafe (opposite Wavertree playground) and the Holyoake Hall. Alight at Penny Lane/Allerton Road. Here is 'The shelter in the middle of the roundabout', 'The barber showing photographs' (Slavin's hairdresser) and 'The banker on the corner' (TSB plc). Opposite is St Barnabas church, where Mike was married in 1982, and Paul was a choirboy in 1954. To the right of St Barnabas is Penny Lane itself, which has Dovedale Towers (St Barnabas church hall) near the middle, and Dovedale Road off it.

Back at the roundabout, proceed up Church Road, and second on the left is Newcastle Road. Number 9 was John's first home, between 1940 and 1945. Nearby is Mosspitts Lane school, the Abbey Cinema and 12, Arnold Grove, where George was born.

Return to the roundabout and board a number 5 bus to Menlove Avenue. Alight at the junction with Beaconsfield Road. Opposite is John's favourite park, Calderstones. Walk up Menlove Avenue, across Vale Road to number 251, Menlove Avenue, John's home for nineteen years. Retrace the route to Beaconsfield Road, and two hundred yards up on the right is the old red gate for Strawberry

Field. DO NOT ENTER THESE GROUNDS.

Carry on up Beaconsfield Road to Church Road, at the top on the right. Cross Church Road, and a hundred yards down is Reynolds Park, a Lennon haunt when he was seeking peace and quiet. Further down Church Road is St Peter's Church, where John was a choirboy. Opposite, behind the single-storey school building, is the large St Peter's Church Hall, where John and Paul first met in July 1957.

Once more down Church Road, to its junction with Allerton Road, turn right and walk along to Quarry Street. At this junction are Woolton Baths, where John was a member of the Swimming Club. In Quarry Street are the remains of Woolton Quarry, from which The Quarrymen derived their name. (Beatles books usually suggest erroneously that the name came from Quarry Bank School). Along Allerton Road, where it becomes dual carriageway, is 120a, Allerton Road, a former home of John's two half-sisters Julia and Jackie, where John was a frequent visitor.

From here one can return to the village for refreshments before proceeding to Speke, or continue along Menlove Avenue and board a bus to return to the city.

If continuing to Speke, take a bus from the village and alight at Western Avenue. The McCartney family lived at number 72 between 1947 and 1953. Nearby is Stockton Wood Junior School, which was attended by Paul. Walk along Central Avenue to Little Heath Road, turn in and on the right is Alderwood Junior School. Opposite is Upton Green where George lived, at number 25, between 1950 and 1962. Behind Alderwood School is another old home of Paul, 12, Ardwick Road.

From here, return to Central Avenue and thence to city by Merseybus.

TELEPHONE NUMBERS FOR INFORMATION

British Rail.. 0151 709 9696
Liverpool Airport... 0151 486 8877
Liverpool YMCA.. 0151 709 9516
Manchester Airport... 0161 489 3000
Merseybeatle Convention... 0151 236 9091
Merseybus Information Line... 0151 254 1616
Merseyside Tourist Office.. 0151 709 3631 or 0151 708 8854
Merseytravel 0151 236 7676
National Express.. 0151 709 6481
The Beatles Story (Albert Dock Complex).. 0151 709 1963